UNSPOKEN WORDS FROM A DADDYLESS DAUGHTER

(a Diary of a Broken Dream)

Written with Jamaya Walker
Edited by Montayj

Published by Jones House Publishing
© 2018
All Rights Reserved, JHP

ISBN-13: 978-1717478320
ISBN-10: 1717478328

Jones House Publishing
joneshousepublishing@gmail.com
daddylessdaughter2016@gmail.com

Daddyless Daughters: Changing My Destiny, Inc.

Acknowledgments

I would like to first give glory to God for making this all possible and allowing me the opportunity to create this book because without him none of this would have happened. God, you continue to bless me even when I feel alone. You always grant me favor and grace and I thank you from the bottom of my heart. Thank you to my mother for continuously supporting my dreams since the beginning of time. You are superwoman; there has never been a moment where you were not there to cheer me on, and I appreciate you so much. Thank you for never forcing me to hide the pain I was and still feel from my father being gone. Mom, I cannot thank you enough for molding me into the woman I am today and encouraging me to push forward and accomplish anything my heart desires. To Mr. Roberts (Montayj), thank you for taking me under your wing my freshman year of college and being a father figure to me ever since. You are a great professor as well as mentor, and I am so honored to have you. To my R.A.W Talent family, it all started with you. Thank you for supporting my dreams to help daddyless daughters through writing and mentoring, you all are amazing people and I am so glad poetry brought us all together. To my best friend, thank you for loving me unconditionally and being my spiritual warrior, "No matter what. Through thick and thin. Forever and always…"

Open Letter

To the young women who have joined together in this book to express years of heartache that they have held captive inside, I just want you to know I am proud of you. I am proud of you for standing in your truth. I am proud of you for speaking out after decades of being silent. I am proud of you for understanding that although your life may not be perfect because daddy wasn't there or because Superman was taken all too soon, that you still found the strength to push forward in life. I am proud of you for blossoming into the amazing women you are today and using your story as your platform for greatness. I am proud of you for starting your journey to heal the awful wound daddy left you with and no longer choosing to hide it. It is okay to cry sometimes and even feel moments of anger because you are human, but always remember that both God and I love you unconditionally. You did not go through this storm just for you nor did you go through it alone. You went through it so that you may help another young lady who is suffering and feels she has no way out or that no one seems to understand her pain. You went through it so that you may help her get through the harsh reality that comes with daddy being gone. And you went through that storm with God holding your hand even when you felt He too might have abandoned you. He didn't. And He won't. You are one resilient, beautiful, intelligent, and powerful woman. Don't allow daddy's absence to negatively impact you because who said being a daddyless daughter was a bad thing? God gives his hardest battles to his strongest warriors and my love you are that keen warrior. Allow God to continue to be your strength on the good days and even on the bad days. Keep your head up Queen you can still make a masterpiece with the scraps you were given!

Love,
Jamaya M. L. Walker

"Once a girl with scars, NOW a woman with a testimony" – J.W

Contents

Open the Diary:

Scars #1

Jamaya Walker
'I been looking for you'

March 28, 2011,

Jamar,
I been looking for you
March 14, 2014 at 3:00 p.m I met you at Applebee's
You walked in 20 minutes late, casually,
One hand in your pocket looking side to side as if this wasn't
a moment that could change our history
My mother told me to go in with no expectations
Keep my dreams behind metal bars and my heart on locked-down
So I kept my head down
Afraid to look up and see my own reflection because
I have the same face as the man I can't trust
With the same deep black hole in my chin
that everybody thinks is beautiful.
But it's just a constant reminder of a dark childhood
Moments later I heard a little boy's voice sound like
wind chimes scream sister
He ran to me
As he wrapped his 9- year- old arms around my torso,
he began asking 21 questions
"Where you been?
How old are you?
You got a boyfriend?
You bet' not have no boyfriend!"

Jamar,
These were the questions that you were supposed
to ask me but you stood there silently
As I stared at the wall trying to fight back uncontrollable tears
You see, eating lunch with a stranger is awkward,
But it's even more painful when that stranger is your father
My brother looked up with confusion and asked you why was I crying

You said nothing,
But your eyes said it all
How you cheated on your wife with my
mother and labeled me an accident
How you were present at his birth but absent at mine
Or how my brother and I share the same
DNA with different last names;
You told me you wanted to build a father-daughter
relationship after 17 years of being absent
As our food arrived I couldn't even eat
My stomach tangled around a knot of hope rising in my throat
You pointed to your forearm
Where my name, birthday and zodiac were tattooed in dark blue
Stretching from the middle of your arm to your elbow
As if you were there when I forced my way out
from between my mother's legs
I guess that tattoo is supposed to be your form of my birth certificate
I don't see how you can have me carved inside of your
flesh yet I can only remember 7 times you embraced me.

Jamar,
You still play hide and seek with your manhood
You carry my name around on display but every year when
April 12 rolls around you change your number
so I can't ask you for anything
But all I wanted was your time
Because you can't put a price tag on my disabled heart.

Jamar,
When you look at your arm do you really
think of me or is that tatt just for show
Just like you brag about me being a poet
Being on 106.1
Performing in front of more than 10,000 people
But you haven't been to not one of my sold out poetry shows.

Jamar,
That day at Apple Bee's you vowed to be there for me
"Jamaya, I want to become a better man"
But 4 weeks later, April 12, 2014,

You changed your number again
That small blood diamond of hope I had was shatter.

Jamar,
I would rather have my tongue cut out of my mouth
before I ever refer to you as daddy
And lynched before I ever tell you I love you
I am done trying to find answers on the crust of your
lies and acceptance on the outline of that tattoo.

Jamar,
I heard you can't erase tattoos you have to cover them
Just like you can't erase me so you tried to cover me up and hide
Many men have to cover the names of their
first loves when things fall apart
Turning past women into black roses blooming on defeated necks
But how many men do you know that have to
cover the name of their firstborn child with
black roses that they never watched grow
I know one…

You…

Jamar…

I am done.

Scars #2

Hadera McKay

Hello reader, my name is Hadera McKay, I am fifteen years old, and I am the only girl of my father's nine children. There is absolutely no question, absolutely no doubt that this is my story, but not mine alone. Every person in my story has a story of their own, and however they may intertwine or stand opposite to mine, it is theirs to tell, and never will be mine. So, when you lay your head to rest tonight, thinking about these stories and what they mean to you, understand that whoever plays a part in your story, has an important story to tell themselves, and please, ask yourself, what part you will play in it.

Diary, as you may well already know,

When I was younger, my father used to creep into my room late at night, sit on the edge of my bed, and whisper that he was sorry, for what, I did not know. I only nodded my head and accepted the apology, not thinking twice, or even once for that matter, knowing that Daddy was sorry, Daddy was so sorry. I believed him with my heart and soul, knew that the silver water rimming his eyes was genuine, and that the warmth of him on the edge of my bed was a comfort I'd never take for granted. I felt it as an everyday occurrence. That my father would always be there, to patch up whatever wrong he'd committed, that I knew nothing of, that his whispered words of sorry targeted for me in the darkness would be my beginning, middle, and end forever, as plot twists were unknown by the first grader who stuck to her stubborn Junie B. Jones and Star Belly Sneetches. Yet, I wasn't so ignorant that I didn't notice the cold on the edge of my bed in the morning sunlight, the chirping birds replacing the quiet lull of my father's

words, the silent calm replaced by a lethal awareness that I was alone. Yes, my father was sorry, Daddy was so so sorry.

Sorry?

Sorry.

Sorry!

I developed a bad habit of saying the word, 'sorry,' when my father left us. I'm sure my mother thought it just another momentary habit of a devloping seven-year-old, and if she thought that, I'm sure I did too. I would apologize for the simplest things, from dropping a pan on the kitchen floor to forgetting to write my name on my homework. I apologized so much, in fact, that the worth of the apology began to mean nothing to those I gifted it to. My mother would have screaming fits at me for saying those two words. Ironically, I had nothing to say to these fits but "I'm sorry." And in the tussle of my mother's frustration, I soon couldn't remember what it felt like to have my father's callused fingers wrapped around mine, or remember what it felt like to sit next to my father watching football. And though I know she didn't mean to, or even know that she was doing it, my mother did a very good job of making me forget my father, in more ways than one.

In the days following my father's leaving, my mother did nothing but work and distracting herself as much as she could with my two brothers and me. My grandmother had permanently moved in with us, as my mother realized she couldn't do much alone. After all, that's what she had divorced my father for anyways, for not doing enough in our lives, for being absent while living with us. So there we were, a family. I did not feel broken, or cross, or any of the other things people said they felt after their parents divorced. But there was a hole in my life, the place on the corner of the couch where my father always sat, that me and my brothers couldn't bring ourselves to sit in for months out of fear that his booming voice would come traipsing down the hallway, telling us to get out of his

seat. Fear. There was a fear in us so strong that we couldn't imagine when it had been built, when it began to dictate every movement we'd thought we'd made alone.

Next day,

I sit on my bed. My stuffed animals lay in disarray around my comforter, as I stare at the wall across from me. I stare and stare, attempting to materialize something to fill my empty stomach. Maybe mama could make me something, I think. No, I shouldn't bother Mama, she's tired. I have to give her time for the dark circles around her eyes to disappear, I think. I wish I could wipe them away for her, and that they would never appear again. Maybe I could ask Daddy to make me something, I think. No, remember the last time, I think. No, I can't do that again. I'm so hungry, I think. I wonder if he remembers the last time, I think.

Thursday, 10:03 a.m.

Fear became my best friend. It sang me lullabies when I couldn't fall asleep, told me to ignore the pounding in my thinning stomach when all I wanted was to eat, and gave me baths and sent me to sleep before my parents could yell at me to do so myself. But through the fog there was a clearing, a chance for me to be free from self-doubt, disgust, and scorn; free from every lie I fed myself in pursuit of silence. Image. Father. Lips moving. The shape of words.

Thursday, 8:30 p.m.

My father is Jamaican. He left Jamaica when he was twelve years old, to meet his own father in the small town of Lufkin, Texas. Jamaica is a country of tradition, spurred from the slavery and oppression of the British on Jamaican territory. To the islander, identity is important, along with the need to make the public see you as well-balanced, stylish, and overall perfect in any way possible. Anything can be seen as weak in Jamaica, from the way you walk, to the job you've chosen to hustle with, or the words that you choose.

The fear of weakness is something that ultimately followed my father all his life and he attempted to make sure it followed me and my brothers as well. The worse form of weakness in Jamaica is public weakness. There is not a day that goes by that I don't hear my father's voice in my head telling me not to do this and not to do that because what would people think. Eventually, this is what freed me. When we went to church or a family gathering my father would act like we were all a big happy family, that my mother wasn't crying herself to sleep at night, that his kids weren't starving while he sat on the couch watching football with a plate of grilled chicken, and that our perfect family life wasn't a nightmare. That fear of public weakness did give me a sliver of hope for my father, but it was washed away immediately once we got back home and the yelling ensued. Sadly, these were the memories that struck me when my father left, not the good, but the bad ones. They played over and over again in my mind like a corny song, until I couldn't remember much of anything good about my father anymore.

Sunday night,

In truth I have only lived eight years without my biological father, two years without a father in general, as my mother remarried, and we were blessed with a new man in our lives. Though this is true, with the negative memories that clouded my head, I began to reconsider the first seven years I had with my father, and came to the conclusion that they did not measure up to these eight years after the divorce at all. There is a thin line between my life—before the divorce, and after the divorce—and inside that line there is a small pocket of time where my father's opinion held more sway than my mother's, where my under twenty-four hour weekend visits with my father amounted to more leverage, power, damage than anything my mother could have done in that week. There was never a tug of war between my parents about who would get us when, or who would go where, and as I grew older I realized that there was

no fight, no push for our weekend visits on my father's end, because he did not truly care. You can't fight with someone who isn't even in the ring.

One weekend,

I hopped out of the truck. My athletic shorts were stained from a soda I had spilled. I wiped it down before skipping to my mother's side in my new tennis shoes. New shoes were rare when I was six, so we had to have bought them yesterday for a good reason. I had no idea where we were going, Daddy just told me to wear something comfortable, and put my new tennis shoes on, so I did. Now, I looked up and saw a few kids my age, stretching their arms and legs weirdly on a patch of grass, Daddy hit me on the shoulder and told me to go join them, I jogged over and a really tall girl led me through the stretches, and when I asked her why we stretched, she said, "Iit's always good to stretch before you run so you don't pull a muscle." I nodded though I didn't understand anything she'd just said. It was then that I noticed a bright red track was surrounding the patch of grass we stretched on. After stretches I ran over to my parents, and Mom and Daddy patted me on the shoulder and made me promise to try my best no matter what. I automatically promised and they pushed me back over to where the other kids lined up to do what I would soon learn were track drills.

Tuesday,

I ran summer track for five years, but right after the first, my parents divorced, and I was faced with a choice. Would I continue in the sport that my father chose for me? Would I still let my father have control over me? Would I still tell him that I got the fastest two-hundred time that day, that I beat two girls in the four-hundred-meter dash, looking for his approval and praise? Would that be a betrayal to my mother? No matter what they say, running hurts, almost as much as having a father that you believe, does not love you.

In the fight against who I was and who I would be, my father became the barrier, the referee; always blowing his whistle and

stopping the brawl from getting too rowdy, too aggressive, too telling. The real champion would be hidden in the crowd, buried under the yes sirs and no sirs that I delivered to my father out of desperation. I would have whole, solid days of confidence, where I asked my mother for anything I wanted without anxiety, where I looked into the mirror at myself, with admiration, only to have a single phone call, or a blunt text message from him, dragging me down into myself once more. There was this internal struggle between what he wanted me to be, and what I wanted me to be, and when I quit track and field, I won something in that struggle; I won something back.

One Wednesday, away from the days of his being there,

Through the years, I ignored phone calls, text messages, scolding conversations, from the man that I did not believe in anymore. He had a new wife, a new life, and at the visits I soon came to just acknowledge as court mandated, no emotional attachment. I closed the bedroom door and thought and thought. I had another brother, a stepbrother. He is an adult now, and in all of his nineteen years of living, he never once got anything from our father that wasn't already owed to him. My father's high school sweetheart raised my father's son by herself, with no help except for a government extracted fee from my father's bank account. In some questioning part of my head, I thought maybe that's what being a father was, monthly fees replacing the gaps in life where a father should have been. Fatherhood was replaced with over the top birthday parties, when a cake and a Dad would have been just fine, summer trips across the country, when a fishing trip and a father were truly the only things needed. Maybe a father was a man who didn't take the only TV in the house upon his leaving because he knew that his kids needed it more than he did. The definition of a father molded and mushed together inside my head, until suddenly, I had one standing right in front of me.

My stepfather is a man so different from my father that you must wonder if my mom was trying to find the complete polar opposite in him. He is giving and confident, kind and generous in a way that my father knew nothing about. Yet there are moments where we still have quarrels with him, just as we did with my father; where my mother reminisces about the few years where it was just her and her kids against the world, with no man to dictate moves or ideals in our lives. And those memories are just that, memories, because my mother knows that without a strong backbone for a family, everything will collapse. Needless to say, we all had to make an effort to rely on a man again and in the midst of that change, and in making a new life, I had to figure out who exactly I was. Identity. Image. New father. Love.

In light of my new life, I always seemed to be comparing it to the life I had with my father. When we would go out to eat, my stepfather would say something like, "If it's in the refrigerator, you can have it," and I would just think of all the times I sat in my bedroom terrified that if I came out to get anything out of the kitchen my father would be right behind me, scolding me for doing something I had no business doing. As I'm writing this, I am now understanding that that was a completely irrational fear, but I'm told that kind of fear blooms from irrational situations. And now, here is this guy telling me I can have whatever I want if it's in the kitchen. These contrasts often stuck with me for days at a time, fostering a resentment that was hard to fight off during my happiness in this new life. But then, I'd go over to my dad's house after weeks of trying to get together, and be faced with another feeling, sadness. My father had a new house, a wife, a dog, everything that it seemed he just couldn't have with his children in the picture. He was happier without us.

This is the part where I choose who I am going to be in life, where I assess my situation, and every situation before it that led me to this place of choosing. This is the place where I either let

resentment consume me, live out a happy life and cut my dad out of the picture every chance I get, or forgive him, and take those weekend visits in stride, understanding that my father's internal problems can't always dictate how I feel about him. But, me being an avid reader and thinker, I like to think that there are always more than two choices in life, especially when it comes to my father.

Three nights ago,

Now I can't say that I don't wake up sometimes in the middle of the night, reaching out to the edge of my comforter for something, someone, to hold on to. I can't tell you that I don't pine after boys who may never like me out of sheer misjudgement. And, I can't tell you that I don't balk at the sight of my father's features staring back at me when I look at my brother, nor can I tell that the resentment I had for my father is completely gone or will ever go away. But what I can tell you is one day, not long ago, my father snuck into my room for one of the last days of my childhood, and said with tears in his eyes,

"I'm sorry baby. I know I've said and done some things that hurt you. I was in a bad place, still am. Me and your Mama were in a bad situation, and you know Daddy has some problems he needs to work out. Daddy just wants you to know that he loves you. You know I love you right? I love you very much, and Daddy is sorry, Daddy is so so sorry for everything he has ever done to you."

That was four years ago. Four years before my middle brother moved in with my father. Four years before my father then adopted five foster children, all boys, who I visit as much as I can, who I speak to, sing to, pray to, and infuse my hope into. Who I rock to sleep at night and direct my love to. Because, with these five children my father is getting a second chance, a chance to be the one who takes his sons on fishing trips in quiet forests, a chance to be the one with the cake and the gift for his son at every single birthday party, a chance to be a father, even if it isn't to another daughter. And, with every prayer, every song, every tentative rock,

I'm making sure he gets it right this time.

Jazz Claiborne

Journal entry #129

Oct. 12th, 2010:

I've never spoken this aloud to anyone:

My dad used to beat me and my mother regularly. He drank a lot, especially on Fridays and Saturdays, and my mother, because her own father had been an abusive drunk and she watched her mother stay, always forgave dad. Drinking made dad an angry, unlovable man. His rationality, whenever the cup went to his lips, was about as stable as trying to stop a dog in heat from interacting. My mother's loyalty to him made me question her toughness and sometimes I felt I hated her just as much as him.

In elementary, mother hid her eye scars with black sunglasses. In intermediate school, she would send me to my grandmother's when her and my dad got into it. He never hit her in front of me, but I could always tell by their uneasiness and quiet when I was in the room. When I made it to junior high his violence spiraled out of control. His drunkenness grew like the New Orleans summer's heat and he would yell at us for everything. If I didn't make my bed at a certain time he would yell. If mother wasn't feeling well enough to cook he would yell. If I wanted to watch cartoons on Saturday, he would yell because he had invited some of his buddies over to watch college football and drink beers. If I was late for school he would yell until I was in tears, calling me a dummy. It became so routine and embarrassing that I didn't bother to tell anyone about it. I didn't talk to mother, even when I saw scars around her neck. She hid it with a scarf, but it was summertime, so everyone knew something was wrong, especially when many of them used the same tactic.

The worst of it came after dad lost a promotion opportunity because he had been drinking on the job. He took it real hard, being

as he was barely making above $19,000 per year to begin with. About a week later, when his drinking on the job didn't cease, he was fired. He blamed me and mother for causing him so much stress that his only outlet was to drink himself into another world. He squeezed my arm before bed until mother begged him to let me go. Because I didn't cry, he pushed me into the wall.

"I can't stand ungrateful children," he yelled, spit flying from his large mouth.

I had to take that insult or urge him further, though I didn't know what I had been ungrateful for. He and mother argued deep into the night that night. It is what put me to sleep. Their arguing. Their unhappiness. Their sad, little, broken marriage. Our unhappy home.

"Before I spend another dime on you I will leave…" Perhaps mother brought up our need for a new couch again.

"You make me hit you…" I'm sure from mother's reminder of her blackened eyes.

"I can do without you and that child of yours…" Mother reminding dad of me overhearing.

It is also what woke me back up.

A bump against the wall.

Bam!

I jumped up quickly.

Bam!

It came again. I followed it with my eyes. I knew where it led. I climbed out of my window and ran to the baseball park across the street from our home. I sat under the bleachers and cried, angered at my dad, angered at my mother for staying with him, angered at myself for being too young to do anything. When I made it back home I could still hear them fighting. I crept by their bedroom window and just stood there, crouched down, listeing to dad call my mother and me horrible names.

I crawled back into my window and pulled the covers over my face, hoping dad would fall out from the liquor he had consumed

ealier and give up his mission. But all that came was the loudest thump against the wall of the night.

Thud!

I felt it in my body. I tipped down the hallway, shaking all the way to my bones. Their door was wide open. What I saw is the broken pieces that belonged to unreality. The monstrous face of abuse. I'd never seen it so raw before, I'd only seen the aftermath of mother in glasses or the scars on her back and neck. I'd only seen him beat me when he felt like it. Before, dad being mean enough to hit mother was a dream, a lie, now it was real. If I could have given all my burdens of sight to God I would have given them away right then and there and walked away. But I was mentally unable to. And God didn't seem to sense my disability either. But even God couldn't falsify what my eyes reflected: mother was being restrained against the cold walls by her neck, body weak as she stood submissively, awaiting her fate, unable to struggle herself free.

"I will kill you," I heard dad tell her. "I will kill you and nobody will care."

"I can't breathe," mother struggled.

I walked to the kitchen as quickly and as quietly as I possibly could, feeling like a superhero. I was rattled by the image of mama's body being gobbled up by dad's big, physical presence. However, fast my heart beat or quickly my feet moved, I didn't move as fast as I wanted because of the weight of the image. My mind went in and out, like signaling flash lights. In between this time, I had managed to reach my hands into the sink and grab the knife mother had used a few hours before to cut tomatoes and onions for the hamburgers she cooked for dinner.

I rushed back to the front part of the house. In my mind I feared walking back to their room, losing my superhero feeling, but I knew that I had to despite the consequences. And I took it on—a tough mission done so I could drive away the sadness from mother's glassy eyes. And even though I did not see her eyes that night, I

knew what populated them: fear, pain, tears, plea. With the knife firmly gripped in my right hand, I addressed my dad: "Let her go before I cut you."

The words rolled weakly from my tongue, like they were looking behind themselves for reassurance. This apparent flaw, I believe, made my dad question his hearing. He looked at me for a still second before asking what I said. I repeated it with more demand: "Let her go before I cut you!"

My dad gazed at the knife in my hand and saw death, or at least that's what I figured he saw because death is what that knife was meant to bring. He let her go and walked towards me. I started thinking about our life and I could see glimpses of poverty and how it had been chewing dad's mind; mama at work all day cleaning buildings for the rich uptown; dad sweating at the sandwich shack; me at home being babysat by my dad's sister who hated me as much as I think he did—staring out of a depressing window, hungry; a condensed space in the house that took away privacy; hot and frustrated because the fan in the window blew in only heat from the outside.

I waited for his predatory approach, and when his evil air began to overshadow me, my grip on the knife tightened. My dad grabbed me by the shoulders but it was a weak grip, feeling perhaps that I did not have the heart to do anything with the knife, that I would drop it and limp off like a three-legged dog. But the tears I could see even in the dark falling from mother's eyes wouldn't allow me. I made a swift move that caught my dad by surprise on his arm and repeated the action two more times, cutting the lower part of his stomach.

All the while mother was leaning against the wall, mumbling, "Stop it, stop it."

I felt a hot liquid on my hand and I knew that I penetrated but the liquid was only a few measly drops, so I also knew I hadn't penetrate my dad's skin deep enough. I desired only to get rid of

him, an avenge for all the times he struck mama when they were alone, for all the times he put her down, for all the times he cracked open that whiskey and went into one of his drunken rages on me and mama with his words. But I'd did nothing, really, because we were still struggling, and I felt like a failure.

My dad finally got the upper hand. He pushed me backward into the living room, grabbed me roughly with both of his rough hands on each side of my waist, and slammed me onto the couch.

"Bring it!" he yelled at me.

He punched me in the head. It dazed me. The knife slid in between the couch pillows.

"Bring it!"

It all happened so quick. After the third time he struck me mother rushed into my rescue.

"Stop hitting her! That's your daughter!" My mother yelled.

Dad didn't care. He pushed mother away from him and she hit the television and went to the floor. I found the knife again. Dad pulled me from the couch and held me in front of him so he could yell some more. He pushed me back as he talked, until we were in the kitchen. He stood in the doorway; my mother joined me next to the refrigerator, all three of us breathing hard. I clung to mother's night dress, sniffling, half afraid, half ready for war. Dad flicked on the light switch; fresh blood stuck to the wall in each place his cruel fingers touched for as long as it could before sliding down the wall. He had a rage in his eyes that could have frozen fire if looked into long enough. Through blank, fearless eyes, dad tried to melt us with his stare. He placed his brutal hand on his stomach where the cherry blood continued to flow, raised it up, showing a work-worn hand dripping and moist, and flung what remained toward me and it landed mostly on my chest, a few drops on my left cheek, simultaneously talking out of anger: "This ain't nothing…," two, three times…a similar action repeated.

He grabbed mother again by the hair. She yelled and struggled.

He punched her in the mouth and the blood flew. She was being tossed around the kitchen. I was standing there, twirling the knife and crying. He was on top of her beating her in the face, so I lunged at him and cut him across the neck. He toppled over, holding onto the wound. Blood was gushing everywhere. Mother was in a panic.

"Jazz! What did you do? Call 9-1-1, Jazz!" she yelled as she went to check on her wounded husband, forgetting her own wounds.

But I didn't. I wanted him to die. I wanted all of the blood in him to come pouring from that wound. He tried to talk, to stay alive, and mother, beaten and bleeding, was right by his side to help him. I wanted to stab him again, but I didn't. I don't know why I didn't. I didn't want him around anymore. He deserved to die and leave me and mother alone.

But he lived.

Mother stayed at the hospital with him until he healed. No charges were filed, against him or against me, but the police hung around for a few hours asking a bunch of questions. Mother asked me to come to the hospital and apologize to him but I wouldn't. I came only to check on her. I had moved in with my one of my aunts the very next day because I knew it wasn't safe for me at home anymore. When dad came home he was nice to mother for awhile, until she nursed his injuries back to 100 percent. He divorced her not long after. I was still twelve. I haven't talked to him since.

Anonymous

Dear Diary, do you remember?

As the three of us walked up the steps, our dad could hardly raise his hand to knock before my Aunt Johnnie flung the door open. She greeted us with warm kisses and squeezed my dad with a comforting hug. Scooting us along to the sitting room where my Uncle was seated watching television, he had no facial expression as he sat there and seemed to soak it all in as my dad and aunt exchanged small talk. Finally, my uncle rose from his seat and shuffled over to the television to turn down the volume as he hesitated for a second to hear the last of the evening news segment. My uncle breathed in deeply, annoyingly, cleared his throat and asked sternly, "Can I beat em?" My aunt and dad looked confused. He repeated, "They can only stay in my home if I can beat them." My dad, having no other choice, replied in almost a whisper looking in my uncle's eyes, "Yes, you can beat them."

By this time my aunt had us occupied with cookies and juice. When I was small, my life was wonderful and my aunt and uncle treated us with loving care. We were fed, bathed, clothed and had shelter. All of our needs were met. The first set of innocent years was filled with joy and love surrounded us.

But maybe those years were only weeks because all of a sudden, one chilly night while washing dishes, I felt a bull whip slap me across my back. I dropped a glass plate from my wet fingers. With shattered glass all over the floor I remember how shocked I was and my first instinct was to dart around the kitchen as the end of the whip seemed to know my locality, striking me again. Everywhere I bobbed and weaved with my bare feet on that cold kitchen floor, the end of the whip was there before I was. Initially, not realizing what was happening, all I could hear was my uncle ranting and raving about how the dishes were not dry and we had better wash every dish in the cupboard all over again.

As he screamed, my sister and I cried tears that seemed to never stop. My foot was bleeding from a deep cut from the glass on the floor. Since my uncle did not seem to care my older, adoptive brother, Victor, picked me up and cleaned the area and then gently bandaged my foot.

This was only the beginning of the abuse we would endure for years to come. My sister and I couldn't do anything right in my uncle's eyes now. If we didn't dry the dishes thoroughly we got a beating, if we went outside we got a beating, if we didn't clean our rooms we got a beating.

My aunt and uncle had a group of foster kids and adults that they took care of and they also owned a few rent houses. My uncle was always a very angry man, possibly from all the activity around the house. When he got mad he would take it out on everybody that came over to the house. One day a guy came over to the house to let my uncle know that he didn't have his rent money for the month. Consequently, my uncle got mad and shot at him. The entire neighborhood was afraid of my uncle because he was such a violent old man.

Although he was a deacon on the deacon board at our church, he smoked cigarettes, chewed tobacco, cussed, and did whatever he wanted outside of scriptures. His body odor reminded me of stale air. I don't know if it was because he was a logger and worked out in the woods all day, or if it was just a mixture of smoke that lingered in his clothing. Since my aunt was not able to take care of herself, he was also her caregiver. Each night he came home from working to help her bathe; she was totally dependent on him.

We attended church often as a family; everybody in the house was expected to go to church. Bible quotes were quoted in daily conversation, but especially when we were being yelled at or getting a whipping. Church was really a safehaven for me because everyone seemed to wear a mask there. My uncle seemed much nicer than he did at home. He played the part well when were around the other

church folk. As faithful members we were in church all day long. One of my favorite scriptures was Psalms 100. We sung in the choir, on drill team, we were quite active in church on a regular basis. As I remember those times in church, I became strengthened in my faith even at such a youthful age.

Dear Diary,

Playing pretend was something my sister and I loved to do growing up. In the hot Texas summers we would cool off by playing in the water. Mostly, we loved to pretend to cook. We could play in mud and water for hours, especially when our uncle was at work during the day. The boarders in our house would pretend with us sometimes, so we often made them mud pies.

I was around seven years old at the time, during the year the beatings began. My sister and I played all over the house, games like 'hide-and-go-seek' or 'Mother May I?' or 'It.' We had secret hiding places everywhere because it was a big house with a lot activity going on all the time. On one occasion I wandered into one of the old men's rooms to take him a specially made mud pie. As I entered the room he invited me to sit on the bed next to him and watch television. I did, laughing as he pretended to eat the mud pie. Then all of a sudden he pulled me closer to him, and then he pulled my bottoms off. I can still recall the sound of his zipper and the fast pant of his desperate breathing as he raped me, stealing my purity.

Screaming frantically, I called for my sister but she couldn't hear me. He was around 40 something years old, late 40s, I assumed, possibly older; I was a little girl, defenseless and scared. No one came to my rescue when I screamed, not my sister, not my mother, not my dad. *Where were they* is I could think about? Afterwards, all I wanted was to be alone.

After that experience I stayed in my room a lot, and I prayed to God that my mother would come to me and take me away. I called him *Jehovah* instead of God. Once my best friend told me if I called

him by His *personal* name He would bring my mother back and take me and my sister from all of this. I imagined my mother showing up at the front door with a sparkle in her eyes and a smile that could melt the moon. My dad would take my uncle's bullwhip and pop him and the boarder with it before we left.

One time I got angry with *Jehovah*, because over time I ddin't get a response from, and my situation never changed. I just decided this is the way my life was supposed to be. A life without a mother and a father. A life without love. An emptiness that could only be filled by my parents whom at this time did not seem to care about my sister or me.

I never told my aunt and uncle about the incident because I was terrified. Please understand, my uncle was an angry man. I was afraid that something might happen to the man. I would cry every night and pray for my mother to come back and get us but she never came. Anger began to build up in me soon after, and the only reason I enjoyed attending school was because this was a way of escape to get away from the beatings and the man.

At school no one really paid attention to me. They did not see the anger grow, the anger that had not yet boiled over, until one day I was so angry at my teacher that I stabbed her in the hand with a sharp pencil. As she leaned over to correct my behavior, I decided this was my opportunity to show her I was in charge. I peeped downward with my big brown eyes noticing her perfectly manicured nails were resting on the desk. I decided to take the pencil that was resting on my desk and stab her in the hand. She began to scream, yell and got angry. This was the reaction I was used to, and this was the reaction that I needed to show everyone how much I hurt. My little intellect and lips could not verbalize the emotions that I was feeling from a deep dark place in the center of my heart. At such a sweet age, I still knew the consequences of my actions, but I did not care.

Back at home, every day was a beating, every day my uncle found a reason to put his hands on us. I got beat twice for stabbing the teacher. I got tired of the beatings so I ran away. I would be gone for two to three days looking for a brief peace, but eventually my uncle would find me. I never would go very far. Under the threat of a beating, my sister would tell him where I was hiding. I hated my sister for telling him because I didn't want to be at that house with such a mean, violent man anymore. No matter how many times I ran away, he found me and would bring me back home. The torture did not stop, but I kept planning my next way of escape.

I ran away so often, our pastor heard about it and decided to come by our home to check on me. He prayed for me and then tried to demonstrate some comfort towards me by explaining that God loved me and I was in a good home. He had absolutely no idea about the beatings, and I dared not tell him the truth. Would he believe me anyway? Probably not because they thought I had a demon that caused me to behave the way I did. Our pastor's attempt to pray that demon away never worked because this demon was real and was a member of his church. It's the spiritual demons we can pray away, but the physical demons that torture and beat children must be discovered and dealt with by humans. Some revenge can only be dealt with by God Almighty.

Dear diary,

By the time I turned twelve I became fed up with the beatings, so I went in the kitchen and got the biggest butcher's knife I could find and went back to my room with the knife and placed it under my pillow. My sister asked me, "What are you going to do with that knife?"

I stared back at her with fire in my eyes and declared, "Tonight will be the last time Uncle Henry beat on us, because he's dying tonight!"

As we slept, my uncle came to the room, turned the lights on and called for my sister and I to get out of bed to re-dry the dishes because he said they were not dry enough. With agony, we both pushed back our covers and tumbled out of bed. I watched closely as my uncle stood over us with a thick leather belt in his hand, appearing to wait patiently for us to stand up flat-footed on the cold floor. But, before he could hit either of us I screamed at him, letting him know, "Uncle, I love you, I respect you, but if you beat us one more time I will kill you. I will kill you," I repeated, gripping my bottom lip as I stood there with a big butcher's knife held tightly in my grip.

He gazed at me for about thirty seconds that seemed to last a lifetime and told me with an anger that trembled in his voice, "Get out of my house right now!"

I ordered my sister, "Come with me!" but she refused to go. For some reason her refusal to leave with me cut me to heart. I walked away that night feeling empowered but empty. It was a chilly Texas night, about 50 degrees, which was very cold to me because I had on a thin night gown and no socks or shoes on my feet. My sister, thinking quickly, threw me some shorts and a shirt out of our bedroom window, but no shoes. She was not trying to get caught up in the act of helping me out because she understood helping me came with severe consequences.

I walked away in the middle of the night without shoes or even a coat. I told myself that I would walk over to my dad's sister's house; she lived nearby within walking distance. While I walked down that long, cold, dark street, several men passed by yelling at me, telling me to go home. A few of them screamed, "Why you out at this time of the night?" And others yelled, "Girl put some clothes and shoes on!" But of course, none of them actually stopped to assist me in any way.

Dear dairy,

If my dad wouldn't have taken me to my uncle's house that day and agreed that he could beat us, I wouldn't have been beat, I wouldn't have been accused of being a demon by church folk, I wouldn't have gotten raped by a 40-something-year-old man, and I wouldn't have been on that dark street that night.

Chastity J. Fields

Dear Diary,

He threw out all of our things. When she returned, with family in tow, she found that her things and my things were gone. Like last year's Thanksgiving garbage, he discarded my things in search of something with monetary value. I'm sure he sold off each Teletubby without much emotion. I can see his face now. Stone-cold as he traded my toys for ten dollars, cash or product. Happy as he inhaled the dirt he'd won. Ecstatic as his high overwhelmed his body.

My things meant nothing to him, even as an infant. An innocent baby who hadn't asked to be born. He discarded things year after year and moved on with his life. They always seem to move on easily.

I am an afterthought. They don't think of me until it's all said and done. Even then, the thoughts aren't developed. I'm sure he never wondered whether I got cold at night or if my belly was full. I don't think he ever thought of how lonely I felt without even my Teletubby to sooth me. I don't think he ever thought of anyone but himself.

I wonder if I look like him. I would trade my mama's gossip for a description of him. She sends me to Google. I look up a celebrity, and when she's sleeping, I type in his name. I find nothing. I don't know whether he's dead or alive. I don't know if I care. He didn't care about me. Still, I find myself searching.

I ask my mama for stories about him. On the tip of my tongue is a question I wouldn't dare ask: *do I look like him?* I want to know if we look alike. When I look at her, often, I see me. But, I don't see all of me. There are missing pieces. I can't ask. Those pieces destroyed her once.

I stare in the mirror, asking myself if I'm beautiful, if I'm good enough. I get on my knees and I ask God the same question. He answers me, but I don't like what He says. It echoes what society says of me. I let it go. I don't ask Him again.

I stare at the ceiling, thinking about the love that I lost. The love that I missed out on. The love that I never knew. I wonder if it would've changed me. I wonder if it would've made me different.

I lay in bed with arms wrapped around me, pulling me close. I ask him if I'm beautiful. He gives me the answer I've always wanted. The answer I always longed for. The answer I always needed. He stares lustfully, and says, "Yes, you are beautiful," and I take the bait.

I often coax myself because it is the closest thing to being full that I've felt in a long time. My cup appears to be half empty. It has spilled over. Unseen.

I destroy everything in my path. Like a storm, I ruin things as I pass by with ruthless eloquence and grace. I don't even touch it, and it has shattered.

I try to put the pieces back together.

Each piece says something different. But, they all lead back to one conclusion: the problem is me.

Me! Me! Me!

That must be the reason he didn't want us. That must be the reason I carry this blame like a sack of rocks. Heavy on my back, it weighs me down. I'm staring into the dirt. The dirt is my mirror.

When I look in the mirror, my eyes are void and empty. I long to be filled. I have been before, at a time I faintly remember. It was beautiful.

I am filled to the brim. Anger and disappointment pool in my eyes. The tears fall as I stare at my reflection, hoping to find a solution.

I don't find one there.

Below the surface, there she is. She is not him, she is not her. She is misguided, lost.

I crack the mirror, giving myself seven years of bad luck. The bad luck never begins. God loves the number seven. God loves me. He tells me that I have punished myself long enough. He begins my healing when I begin to see Him through the broken mirror.

Like a bandage over an open wound, my scars are patched up. Like the garbage bags he packed with my things, I take out the baggage he left me with, and I leave it on the curb.

I take a few steps away and will myself not to look back. I want to leave it all behind. Screw the reflectioj in that mirror!

This shouldn't be too hard. He was always good at leaving. He knew how to leave everything behind without a care in the world. He knew how to walk away.

What can I say when they ask me?

All I know is what society says, what they echo, the cliché, the response they give to my questioning facial exressions: *father knows best*.

Nicole

Journal entry #11

My father wouldn't listen so I started keeping this journal, the only thing that would offer an ear and not judge me.

I am the product of a daddyless daughter and a daddyless son. Because of that, the importance of a father has never been valued in my upbringing or even throughout my life. I actually forgot a father figure was supposed to be around until someone from school brought it up. Once, in elementary there was an open house. My mom couldn't make it so I didn't attend. The next day in school my classmates wanted to know where I was and I said my mom had to work. Then someone asked, "Well what about your dad?" Up until I was eight, I went to school with other kids who didn't even know who their fathers were, and I just didn't ask questions about that. I figured once my father left my family no one would ask me either, but I got questions all the time. Throughout my life he has been out of town, at work, asleep, sick, in traffic, and even in prison before I finally said that he walked out on us.

I was eight years old when my mother and father sat me and my two older brothers down in the living room for "the talk." My mother was teary eyed, and my father was passive as he began to tell us how things would start to change for all of us.

"Your mother and I are getting a divorce," he said, looking away from us.

I looked around, my second oldest brother was crying and my oldest brother had a look as if he saw it coming all along. I began to smile and even giggle a little.

My mother said to me, "Do you know what this means?"

"No," I said, which was a lie. My mother told me that her and my father would not be married anymore and we would not all live in the same house and things would not be the same. I knew all of

that, but the situation was so tense, I thought maybe an eight-year-old smile and giggle would fix everything; it didn't.

Journal Entry #16

Everyone around me has a father but me, or at least some kind of active father figure who has been around for most of their life that they can call on for whatever needs a father provides. I don't even understand what a father is supposed to do for a daughter because I've never experienced it, and initially I didn't mind because my mother taught me that I could never miss out on anything I never had. But somehow it feels as if one day the world had a Father's Day sale and I didn't have enough to get one.

Journal Entry #17

I didn't realize I was "daddyless" until I saw so many people with a dad.

I wondered, am I even missing out on much? I realize now I am a daddyless daughter, but the extra focus I had to put onto myself that my father did not made me care for myself more. Because my father decided to leave, I'd rather him miss out on me rather than I miss out on him. My father didn't know he would miss out on a high school and college graduate, an honor roll student, a writer, and even a friend when he decided to walk out.

Later in life when I asked my mother why everything had changed, she would say my father left to be with his soon to be second wife and he never came back because he was too ashamed to right his wrong. When my father was asked by my oldest brother why he left, he would say a series of things that didn't make much sense, then it would all somehow boil down to being my mother's fault. That was his response when he first left us, and to my knowledge it hasn't changed. I suppose my brothers got tired of waiting on my dad to make the first step back into all of our lives so they went to him. My oldest brother found a way to get into contact with him. They hung out from time to time and visited for the holidays. In the beginning,

it was just my oldest brother who had a relationship with my dad but then my second oldest visited with him too. I chose to stay in the place my father left me. Some have said over the course of my life that I'm just holding a grudge but to me it's a grudge worth holding. The only thing standing in the way of my father gaining a relationship with me is his tremendous amount of guilt.

Journal entry #19

Up until a few years ago my father was always welcome back to apologize and make things right with me. I felt he should have a chance at having a real relationship with me even through his mistakes. I have a theory that my father leaving his family was the greatest mistake of his life, and everything went downhill for him then and there. In 2014, he was sentenced to three years in federal prison for passport fraud. I never felt like more of a stereotype in my life. My mother was a single parent, I had no relationship with my father and then he was about to serve jail time! I couldn't believe it, the man I barely knew as my father became less and less familiar as I spent more years apart from him, and after that incident, I'd never know him again.

Journal Entry #22

My father still doesn't listen so I continue keeping this journal, the only thing that offers an ear and does not judge me.

Some would say that my father chose a woman over his family, but I believe he chose himself. When people get married they commit themselves to the other person. What was once all about them now becomes a partnership. My parents got married at 22, which means they left college, went back to Houston and started a life together before they truly got to know themselves. After 18 years of marriage and three children I suppose my father wanted to do things for himself. There's a similar pattern in myself, if a situation is not beneficial to me I'll contemplate leaving. In relationships, a guy has

about a half a chance to give me a bad vibe and then I'll just call it quits, no talking, no working it out I just leave, because I think I'm protecting myself from a huge downfall I already saw coming. I have this fear that I will fall in love and be left behind like my mother was.

My relationship with my mother is her telling me not to make the same mistakes she did. "You gotta be careful who you have kids for," a joke she would say when me or brothers do something silly. She always taught me to get what I want out of life first and then marry. Now that I'm 22, not much has changed. She tells me, "I got married at 22 but you don't."

I find it unfortunate that she committed herself to her family despite all the obstacles and was betrayed in the end, so when I have relationships I try to avoid too much commitment, too much trust. I don't expect much from others as well. I don't care to ask for favors nor do I believe I can really depend on others. I'm always expecting someone to let me down, but on the bright side I take rejection pretty well.

When most people think of a daddyless daughter they categorize us all as women with little girl mindsets that make child-like decisions. People assume that daddyless daughters chase their fathers through men they date. The assumptions of daddyless daughters also include poor decision-making, bitterness towards men, and even animosity towards their future daughters. I have been accused of such things due to the lack of a father being around and it's not fair. I never liked or understood the feeling of fault that was placed upon me due to my father's absence. Every emotion I feel was somehow due to his leaving according to anyone who thinks they know about all daddyless daughters. I'm not a victim or a lost cause. I know my father's decisions were ultimately his own and had nothing to do with me being unfit. I wonder sometimes if there are other daddyless daughters like me who also focus more on themselves rather than the people that walk out on them?

Larryisa Thomas

It's ironic to me that I am named after my dad. As I think back on why I was named after him, I assumed it was because I was his, you know. We shared names so we were going to share a bond that could never be broken. I was hoping that he would be the man to show me how I should be treated by every other man out there. Unfortunately, that has not been the case.

My name is Larryisa Thomas. I am from Freeport, Texas. I was raised by my amazing mother and my grandparents. Words do not begin to describe how thankful I am for all they did for me growing up. I attend Prairie View A&M University. I am a Sociology major with an African American Studies minor. The reason I chose to study sociology is because I've always taken an interest in why people do what they do. There are people in this world who may come from the same backgrounds, but tend to follow different paths, and those kinds of actions interest me. I am also learning about African American studies because history, specifically African American, history has always had my heart. It also happens to be another detail my father and I share.

Day 6:

One of the hardest things about being a daddy-less daughter is knowing who your father actually is and knowing that he still refuses to fix his mistake. My dad was around when I was younger. I never lived with him, but his presence was made a few times, even had some good times. When I was in first grade, my mom decided to move us to Georgetown, Texas. At the time, he lived in Austin, literally twenty minutes up the road. I knew who he was, I had his phone number, and I had even been to his house a couple of times. With all this information, I saw my dad once every three months or so.

My relationship with him was immediately undeveloped. I did not know much about him. I do know that he adored my grandmother (his mom). She raised him alongside her husband (his stepdad). I'm not too sure of how his relationship with his stepdad was though. My dad hardly ever spoke of his relationship with his own dad. I remember asking about my grandpa to my mom, because I knew better than to ask my dad, but she had very little to say about him. I've heard stories from her and my aunt but never directly from my dad himself. The common story I've been told is that my grandpa (my dad's dad) was not involved in my dad's life. I remember when I was about ten, my dad had taken me to a funeral. His dad was there and that was the first time I had ever met my grandpa. He and my dad did not really speak to each other. Maybe just a quick hi and bye. Excuses could be made that my dad did not have his own dad around to show him how to be one but that excuse just does not sit well with me. As a father, I'd assume you would not want to put your own kids through a similar heartache if you've dealt firsthand with the pain yourself.

Day 9:

I started playing softball when I was five. I got more involved and started taking it seriously when I was eight. We had practice three times per week, games every Saturday, and soon, tournaments every weekend. I witnessed my teammates arrive to practices and games with their parents but all I could ever focus on was their dad's standing right next to them with their team shirt and baseball hats on. They would coach their daughter's teams, while encouraging them to be better. The dads would yell and cheer for their daughters. All I had was my mom, driving me to practice and tournaments, wearing her team shirt cheering for me. You would hear all these men's voices yelling for their daughters, while my

mom was sitting there successfully out cheering them. That's when I realized that I was always going to have my mother every day of my life, not my dad. It would hurt me so much seeing my friend's dads at the games for them while mine was nowhere around. The question of why was I not good enough popped up into my head multiple times. My mom would always tell me that it was my dad's lost that he was missing out on my life.

Day 13:

From what I was told, my mom and dad were never in a relationship. They loved each other dearly at one point, my mom maybe loving a little bit more than my dad. They had known each other since they were late teenagers. She moved to Austin with him when my older sister was born. When she was pregnant with me, she decided to move back to my grandparent's house. I remember growing up watching my mom and dad "playing house" with us for a few days. Then the house was empty.

Day 15:

I feel like the relationship my mother and dad had interfered with me and my mom having a stronger relationship. While in middle and high school, my mom and I were never really close. We loved each other but we had nothing in common compared to the commonalities I shared with my dad. She would take the anger she had towards my dad out on us. She never just ignored us or stopped loving us, but she did seem to get annoyed with us for the smallest reasons. I used to love it when my dad would call my mom and tell her that he wanted to take me out to go do something. My mom though, would quickly shut him down because in her head, it wasn't fair of him to want to just take me rather than take my brother and sister also. If he could not get just me, then he would change his

mind instead of having to take all of us. I would be so mad at my mom because there were times it seemed like my dad was actually trying and being shot down. I never hated my mom for this, but I never understood it either. My brother and sister never cared to have a relationship with him like I did so why was she going to force their hand? Although these events may have caused some tension between my mom and me, it was never anything serious. This was the woman who was raising three kids on her own so who was I to question her?

Day 18:

The closest thing to a father I had was my grandpa. I didn't get to see him every day growing up because we lived four hours away from each other, but he did fatherly things. He would talk to me about boys, punish me, keep me on top of my school, attend a few of my games, and push me to pursue my dreams. Although he was my "father-figure," he was my grandpa first. I never looked at him as a replacement father because that was something he could never become. He had his own daughters and was their father first. I never looked at or even wanted my grandpa to step up as my father-figure because that wasn't what he was supposed to do. I had my own dad, who just simply choose to not be there every day.

Day 19:

The few times my dad would show up I became a daddy's girl for those brief moments. He would give me all the attention I desired and then some, spoil me with words and taking me places. It was nice not to have to share that attention with my brother and sister. And when my dad would leave my life again, the attention that came with him would leave too.
It made me act out.

The psychological issues I experienced was any guy who gave me the slightest attention, I ran with it. I felt like I needed to keep them around because they were making up for the attention I was not getting from my dad.

I wasn't necessarily dating or engaging in sexual activity with all of these boys, but I was staying up late on school nights and talking to them every chance I got because they were telling me things I felt I needed to hear. My mom had found out that I was talking to these boys all day and at one point even took my phone away.

My acting out occurred mainly during middle school. I wanted to get my dad's attention. When we got in trouble or did things out of the norm, my mom would usually handle it on her own. But this case was different. I was hoping she would see what I was doing and why I was doing it, and would involve my dad. There were times when I wanted him to come punish me and show me he cared about what I did, while there were other times I wanted him to know that I was getting attention from other people, in the hope he would step up and remind me that I should only be getting that love from him. He was supposed to be the number one man in my life. I was naïve to think that he would feel like he had competition.

Day 21:

I lost my virginity at an extremely young age. I did it because of the attention I was receiving from an older guy. I was and still am taken advantage of by certain guys because of my "daddy issues." I would allow guys to do whatever they wanted to me because I was finally being looked at by a male as someone worthy. I have never been a relationship person because I did not allow myself to get close enough to anyone. The first man to break my heart was my dad so I was definitely not going to allow another guy to do that to me. I have been in a few relationships, but they were nothing serious or even lasted long. I tended to think the worse and just prepared

myself for them to leave. I have this idea that they're going to get comfortable and eventually leave me. With the mistrust and the expectation of being abandoned, I do not necessarily go out looking for love from men. I did at one time seek any attention I could get from one, but love to me is something I don't want in my life at the moment.

I was a gullible girl when I was younger. All you had to do is say the right things and you had me. I like to think I was a strong person but I had a weak mind at certain times. When I was sixteen, I was in an abusive relationship. I was with someone who protected me, loved me in the beginning, and was always there for me. I trusted him because I knew there was no way he could hurt me. When he got comfortable and realized he had me, that's when things started to get out of control. He knew all the issues I had with my dad and he used that against me. He would tell me that there was no one out there who loved me like he did, and would continuously remind me that my own dad did not want me. He made me feel like if I wasn't good enough for my own dad then I was not good enough for anyone else. I finally left him after a year, somewhat damaged, but I healed from that pain. I blamed my dad for everything I went through in that abusive relationship. If he had not abandoned me then I would have not felt the need to go out and look for or accept anything from anyone else.

Day 22:

My sexual issues are something that I have kept to myself because I don't feel like there's anyone who can relate to what I go through. There are times I am disgusted in myself because I allow myself to be used for just a simple satisfaction. I never had a father, let alone a male figure talk to me about sex besides my grandpa. My mom rarely did it herself. So I was left to figure it out myself. I learned about sex and my body based off what these boys were telling me. I

was willing to give myself up just because of words I wanted to hear. Sex is something that is supposed to be passionate and be done with someone you love; that's not my case. Having sexual relations does not give me any kind of feelings. I look at it as something that just happens.

My dad has other kids, all around the same age with different women. He has not been in a committed relationship most of his life. I can still see him meeting some of his women friends at his house, while we were left in the living room. I saw what he did and just followed his actions because that's all I knew. I saw him use my mom when it was convenient for him.

Day 27:

For the longest, forgiving my father was not even a thought. He had hurt and abandoned me so he didn't deserve forgiveness? My hate for the situation started around the age of fourteen. I did not want him around at all. I felt like I had gone so long without him and him coming around more would just ruin things. My mom tried her best for us to rekindle our relationship but in my eyes, it was a dead issue. Once in a blue moon he would pop up at my softball games when I was a young teen and actually sit there to support me. I wasn't the one who invite him though. My mom knew the similarities my dad and I shared, such as both of us being stubborn and having too much pride. She figured if neither one of us was going to make an attempt to reach out, that she would do it for us. That caused some problems between my mom and me during my childhood. Of course, seeing my friend's dads there for them every day made me feel sad, but their childhood in the general aspect was different from mine since I had double the support from my amazing mom.

Day 28:

Building up all that hate and anger made me a bitter teenager, but I wouldn't say that my childhood was stolen. The anger I had towards him, I took out on other people. We are a religious family so my mom would always tell me to forgive because I was not hurting my dad, only myself. He was still going on about his day, while I was sitting there with this anger just because I could not forgive. I am the type of person where I do things on my own time. I don't like being told when to move on from something.

I matured somewhat the age of seventeen. That's when I started doing for myself and growing up. It was my senior year of high school, and I had just gotten accepted into college. I was so excited that I ran to my mom and thanked her for pushing me and believing in me all these years. She deserved so much recognition. A few months later, I received a scholarship from my former Head Start. There was going to be banquet held for the recipients. The thought of calling my dad did not run through my head at all. Seeing my families' proud faces made me realize who I was being successful for. I realized that everything I had accomplished in my life was without him. It didn't take a pastor, counselor, teacher, friend, or my mom for me to forgive him; but it took me looking back at all my accomplishments that I did without him for me to forgive the absentee father that I had.

Day 33:

Forgiving my father is definitely a process. Right before I went to college, I had a conversation with him to tell him that I forgave him for all he had done. He did not take the conversation as serious as I had hoped, but it felt like I was relieving so much anger by getting the words, "I forgive you," out. Although the conversation went left, I was happy. I have relapsed though. There have been times where he has popped up and we talked a couple days or even go out

to eat. I get excited because I feel like, "Oh he's trying to have a relationship with me." But I then get disappointed again because he disappeared per usual. His showing up when it's convenient for him causes some pain and makes me regret forgiving him but then I remember how happy I was when I did forgive him.

Forgiveness is never for the other but for yourself. There are girls who have had worst or no relationship with their father whatsoever but still manage to wake up with a smile on their face. There are some girls who are unaffected by not having a relationship with their father, while others have so much anger and pain with the nonexistent relationship. Forgiving your dad could possibly release so much pain in your heart just by getting the words out. In my case, forgiving this man had no impact on him. I'm sure he was aware of the damage he had caused in my life by not being there but he didn't care too much to fix that damage. I had to forgive him for myself.

Day 35:

I've tried multiple times to just ask my dad, "Why? Why was I not good enough for you to be around?" searching for a serious answer, no laughter. My dad does not take any responsibility for the damage he's caused. He says he did nothing wrong. He blames everything on my mom. He strongly believes she is the reason he and I did not have a relationship. To him, my mom and her family has put so much negative things about him in our head that he thought it was pointless to even try to get those thoughts out. He assumed I had an ideal picture of him in my head that it was worthless to even try to show me who he really was. He felt like child support and birthday phone calls was him being a father.

Over the past two years, I have had three conversations with this man trying to understand why he left. One day when both he and I grow up, and can have a real conversation, I want to ask him why

was he not around? Was it because of my mom, or him, or me? I am not going to bash my dad because even though there's tension, I respect him, so first thing first, he is a good man. He just does not know how to put his children first. I would tell him that he missed out on so much of my life because of his own reasons. He would know that I was extremely successful in softball, I stayed out of trouble, I made good grades in high school, was involved in school organizations and my church, mentored young kids, and even made it into college without him. As of now, I fear having kids because I would be scared for my child if their father was not there for them. I see what I went through with being daddy-less daughter, and it would break my heart to see my future kids going through that not good enough stage.

Tierra Taft

Dear Diary:

Please listen to my story; I can't tell it to anyone else.
New Arrival
September 12th, 1993

My mom went into labor, listening to 'Sussudio,' by Phil Collins, and trying to dance her way to getting me to turn with my head down so she could push me out. I apparently was a stubborn baby at times so clearly that didn't happen. I was born by C-section. A healthy baby girl whom they named Tierra. My mom told me that when she woke up, the first thing she saw was me. I was laying down with my hands to my face. I was dressed in all pink with pink booties and a beanie on with a Mickey Mouse stuffed animal by me. My mom told me that she cried when she saw me, that I was the most beautiful thing that she had ever seen and how she couldn't believe that she brought me into this world. She picked me up and rocked me in her arms and sang to me.

In the beginning of the marriage my parents again were happy. They enjoyed each other's company and while living in their comfy apartment, created their own sense of heaven. Sadly, this feeling didn't last forever. My dad started to get irritated with the fact that he was the only one bringing money into the house and still irritated from the fact that he wasn't able to do drugs or drink. He told my mom that it was time for her to go back to work. My mom wanted to go back to work but couldn't because she was still supposed to be on bed rest until her body fully healed from the C-section. My dad felt otherwise. They started to get into more arguments than usual, but my mom brushed it off, letting her body heal properly before going back to working at the clinic.

My parents had one joy in common: they loved taking pictures and videotaping me. Most of my life as a child was captured or recorded by them, like they were making a film with a never-ending

budget, never-ending scenes, and a very patient director. The pictures or videos ranged from me just eating food to my birthday parties and even getting bit by a duck at the park. I knew as a kid that my parents loved me. I knew that my parents only wanted the best for me. They started me off in Pre-K so that I could start learning at an early age. It wasn't until I started Kindergarten that I started to see a change in my surroundings at home. I started to notice that my dad would get mad at us for things that didn't even make sense. Most of the images that happened were so bad that I tried to block them out of my mind and for the most part it worked. My dad was the type that wanted people as well as his friends to think that our family was perfect. He liked to flaunt his money as well as his perfect family to others to show them just how put together of a family we were—my dad with his perfect job of building airplanes at a company while my mom was in nursing school and a daughter that people loved ever so much. People would always come up to my parents and tell them how sweet I was and how they wished their children were like me. People would tell my parents how beautiful our family is and how blessed we were to have that. Though this image was indeed a nice sight, they didn't know what was going on behind the scenes.

Back then we attended a church called Saint Agnes. My dad would sing in the choir while my mom would play the piano with the rest of the musicians and I was put into the children's choir. I personally didn't want to be in the choir but since my parents, mostly my dad wanted me to do it, I did. My dad had his good and bad days. We would be in church and me being a kid, I didn't understand what the preacher was talking about so I would ask my mom if I could draw or lay down. My dad on the other hand didn't play that. I was supposed to listen to the preacher, not draw or go to sleep. I would get whoopings at home after church for doing thing like this. My mom would try and stop him and try to explain to him that I am just a child and that I wouldn't understand what's

going on, which is why they have children's church. My dad didn't want to hear that. I would get whoopings for many things when it came to church, for not paying attention to the pastor during service, playing with my friends when I should be sitting down, not singing loud enough while in choir, not being able to tell him what I learned in church and more. I got a whopping once because in children's church we didn't learn anything. We just colored and ate cookies and orange juice.

Dear diary,
Do you remember the pageant?

At the age of five I was entered into the Delta Sigma Theta pageant. When my mom told me about it and I was actually excited. She told me I had to have a talent in the pageant and that she thinks I should sing since I had such a pretty voice. She asked me what I wanted to sing. I told her that I wanted to sing, 'Tomorrow,' from the movie *Annie*. My entire family was so excited about the pageant. My Aunty Val is a Delta and is the one who got me into it. I remember going to find a dress to sing in. The one we found was so pretty. It was gold and white with gold sparkles and lace on it with little gold strap sandals that my mom bought to go with it. She also got me some gold bangles to wear with it. My mom took me to practice with the other girls I was competing with because we had to learn a group dance for the pageant. We had to do a cute little dance routine to, 'My Girl,' by the Temptations. My mom made me feel so good about this pageant and really bumped my head up to think I could win. At home, we went over the song, 'Tomorrow,' so many times it was crazy. In my house we had a computer/music room. My mom and I would go in there and she would get on the keyboard and play, 'Tomorrow,' while I had the microphone and sang. On the day of the pageant, I was confident and ready to go. My mom told me that I walked into the dressing room with the other girls and I told them I was going to beat them. The pageant

was hosted in a big fancy hotel. The dressing room that we were in was large. It had tall ceilings and enough room for over 30 people in there. Hairspray and clothes were everywhere. The pageant was videotaped. There were so many things we had to do in order to get me ready for the pageant. My mom had to fix my hair and make sure my outfits were ready. Everything went smoothly during the pageant until the talent portion. I watched this girl go on stage and praise dance to this song called, 'Now behold the lamb.' It was so pretty but when it was my time to get on stage I grew a little nervous. I walked up on stage in my little gold and white dress with my black shiny shoes and gold straps, took the microphone and waited for the music to start so that I could sing. My mom could see the nervousness in my face. Luckily, she came prepared. She went to the back of the middle-sized room the pageant was being held in where I could see her perfectly and acted out the words in case I forgot. It was so funny because her acting out the words perfectly made me smile and laugh a little, which gave me more confident. Then in the middle of singing, my microphone stopped working. It was so embarrassing, but I kept singing. The crowd was cheering me on and so was my family who was sitting to the left of me by the stage. My dad ran up and somehow fixed the microphone for me while I was still singing into it, which made our family look amazing because they were helping their little girl. When the song was over, everyone was standing on their feet cheering and clapping for me. I went back into the dressing room with my mom and cried a little because of the nerves but she told me how proud of me that she was and that I did amazing. I put my gold and white dress with my strappy gold sandals and gold bangles up and went to go sit with the other kids from the pageant. The judges were fixing to start giving out awards and announcing the winners. I was called for certain awards but I was mostly playing and talking to a girl I made friends with while they were announcing the winners. My name got called a couple more times so I went on stage but instead of getting

small trophies, I received big trophies that were taller than me. I went to sit back down and finish talking with my friend, then my name was called again. This time everyone was cheering louder than usual. My mom was tearing up and I still didn't understand what was going on until I walked on stage and one of the judges put a crown and sash on me while another judge was bringing up three more trophies. I looked at my mom confused before I realized that I had won. People tookg pictures of me while I was on stage being crowned. They wanted pictures with just me, then pictures with my family. The most famous one that they took was a picture of my trophies sitting around me in a circle but an opening in the front with me sitting in the middle. My family was so proud and happy for me. That day was one of the happiest days I ever had.

Dear diary,

As a kid one of the biggest things I would get in trouble for was sucking my thumb and taking my favorite stuffed animal, BoBo, everywhere I went. BoBo was my favorite teddy bear given to me when I was born. She was my best friend. I would talk to her about everything. I know I should have broken out of the habit of sucking my thumb as a baby but both BoBo, my blanket and sucking my thumb was the only type of security that I felt like I had growing up. When I would get in trouble at church or get in trouble by my dad, I would find BoBo or both my blanket and BoBo and I would suck my thumb until I felt safe again. As I got older I started to drift from my blanket and started to bite my nails to the nubs. Most of the times I would get in trouble is when my mom was at work. I would go to school and my dad made sure he was the top person to contact if I ever got in trouble. I had to show my him all of my progress reports and report cards. Anything less than an A would equal me getting beat and made fun of. My dad would whoop me and tell me that I was nothing and would never be anything in life. That I was ugly and nobody loved me. He would tell me that I

wasn't smart, that I was an idiot, a bonehead and sometimes worse names. It got so bad that I was so afraid of showing him anything from school, even projects. There were times that he would beat me so bad that I would have bruises all over my body and wouldn't be able to sit down in class or even lay down in my bed. I would do what I could to survive in that house. I would try to get on my dad's good side in any way that I could if it spared me from his hand, belt, switch or extension cord. I remember one day that I was coming home from school and my report card was in. He told me to go get my backpack and sit at the dining room table where I normally do my homework. He sat across from me at the circular crown table and told me to let him see my report card. I remember my heart dropping because my grades were good but not good enough for his expectations. I remember I had a couple of A's but I also had a couple of B's and C's. My stomach started to flutter and drop to the floor when he looked at my grades and then looked at me. His eyes were red and I knew that I was in for it. I knew that there was no way around me getting a whooping. I remember he asked me why my grades were the way they were? I told him that I was doing my best but it was hard. He told me that was no excuse. In one of the classes on my report card I had a 98 and that pissed him off too because even though it was an A, in his mind an A was a 100 and nothing less for that class. He told me, "You know why you're fixing to get it right?" When he said that I started to cry as I thought of the pain to follow. I was tired of getting whoopings and I was doing my best, but school was starting to get hard for me. He took me in the back to his room and told me to put my hands on the bed and not to move. With each swing came excruciating pain. He would hit my legs and my butt and my back and if my legs gave out he would hit me again and tell me to stand up before I get more. Sometimes it felt like those beating would last for hours. After he would beat me, he would tell me to get ready to go so that we could go to the gym. My dad always liked to work out. He wanted to be

like those bodybuilders from the magazines. He would take me to 24 Hour Fitness and he would take me to the daycare center in the gym to play until he was done working out. There were days that I had fun in the center but most of the time I was too sore to move or play so I would just go color or watch whatever movie was being played. I wanted to tell my mom what was going on but fear kept me quiet. I was afraid that I would get in more trouble than I was already in. I also feared that no one would believe me so I kept it a secret.

Dear diary,
Why did they hate everything about me?

As a child I would always get picked on for my glasses, or the way I dressed, or for my teeth, or even my name. In Spanish, Tierra means dirt or land, which made for easy game from other kids. Bugs Bunny is one of the many nicknames they bestowed upon me. I got picked on mostly between kindergarten through 2nd grade because of my buckteeth and from sucking my thumb so much as well as having to wear glasses. I would also get picked on because of my clothes. My dad always wanted a son deep down so when we would go shopping he would get me clothes or shoes that were more fitting for a boy, which didn't help me in school. When we would go shopping for clothes, he would always get things that matched so that we could wear them together when we all went out. We had matching jean jackets with jeans or windbreaker jumpsuits. Girls would always come up to me asking me why I have those clothes on or why my glasses look the way they do. I never had an answer.

I was a pushover growing up because I really didn't know how to handle situations like this. It was already enough that I was being physically, verbally and emotionally abused at home. I didn't want the same thing to happen while I was in school too. After school, my mom wasn't able to pick me up right when school let out,

forcing me into an afterschool program called Latchkey. Latchkey was held in the cafeteria where the rest of the kids that had the same issue with their parents picking them up after school would wait. There was this one particular bully that I hated with a passion. She would mess with me just to mess with me. I never knew why but she would always back off once my mom got there. Once, her and her friend took my sweater jacket and threw it on the ground. They laughed and made fun of me, calling me many names and spitting on my sweater. When my mom got there and saw me crying she ran to me asking me what was wrong. I told her what happened and she lost it. The girls that were bullying me tried to act like nothing happened. My mom went to one of the teachers who was over Latchkey and went off. She was yelling and saying that I was her child and that she will not have someone bullying her kid. I got my sweater back and also an apology from the two girls. At that moment, I wanted to tell my mom about my dad, but I always had a voice in the back of my head saying not to, think about your legs buckling, so I didn't.

Dear diary,
It's the junior high days.

There were many days where I was happy in life as a kid. Knowing my mom and dad loved me, I felt blessed even though there were issues. Since my mom was a nurse, she had to take on many shifts that ended up being night shifts or late shifts in general while she was still trying to finish nursing school. Me and my mom used to wake up at four in the morning during weekdays. She would wake me up, help me get dressed and she would drop me off at her friend's house so that she could take me to school while my mom went to nursing school. My dad didn't like waking up early and refused to get up to take me to school so my mom had to make a way in order for me to go. During those years as a kid, I always wondered why my dad was the way he was. Why he would act one

way then another. My mom used to tell me that my dad was part werewolf, that when there's a full moon, he would change into the monster that he is. My dad was the type of dad that only wanted to be in my life when he wanted to show off his family around his friends. The problem was that I wanted him in my life for more than that, and for him to not be so mean. I wanted him to be at every band concert, choir recital, band trip, football game, gymnastics meet, track meet and to wake up to take me to school.

By the time I was in Junior High, things were getting worse with my family. My dad would work out at the gym and stay out all night, causing my mom to leave him. My dad didn't slow down his ways because usually when my mom left, she came back after a few days. I started making friends after my mom put me in a teen camp the summer before I started 7th and 8th grade. I made many friends there and learned many lessons. I started Junior High and learned that I was actually really good in sports. I was fast when running laps, learned how to play a little volleyball and slowly started to try to play basketball. I was also blessed to have the most amazing science teacher in the school named, Mrs. Davis. She knew the situations that my mom and I faced when we would go home. I would stay after school in her classroom with some of my friends who were also close to her. We would listen to music, dance, make jokes, and also learn a few life lessons. Mrs. Davis was the teacher that taught me how to meditate as well as control my breathing when I would get into situations that would stress me out, including dealing with my living situation. During 7th and 8th grade I was slightly weaker in my class subjects because of my dyslexia but she would help me when she could, and I appreciated that. Sometimes after school tutorials my dad would have one of those days where he wanted to pick me up and take me home. One day when I stayed for a tutorial session, my dad came up to the school to try and pick me up. The front office was calling me down so that I could go home. I knew it wasn't my mom coming to pick me up because she

was still at work. When Mrs. Davis went down to the office to spy and see who was there to pick me up she ran back to the classroom. She and my 8th grade teacher Mrs. Cooper came up with a plan to get me out of the school. By this time in my life, my mom had finally gotten away from my dad for good. The judge had already talked to me and my dad wasn't granted visitation because the court felt like I was emotionally unstable to deal with anything that had to do with my dad. Mrs. Davis told me to get my things once she got me to calm down and stop crying. She grabbed her keys and purse and snuck me down the hallways and out the school doors to her car. The whole time I kept panicking because all I could think of is what my dad might do to me if he sees me. Would he whoop me as soon as he saw me because I told the judge what happened? Would he kick me in my back or pick me up and throw me again? The whole way home I was paranoid. I remember the last words that Mrs. Davis said to me, "When you get upstairs, lock the door. Lock both locks and don't answer the door for anyone unless me or your mom calls you, do you understand? You will be okay, sweetie, just go take a nap. It's going to be fine." When I got in the house, I did just what she said. I must have cried for hours.

D. Epps

Make me lovely

"You save yourself or you remain unsaved."
— Alice Sebold

I was born in Amarillo, Texas, and moved to Dallas when I was two years old. My mother and father were never in a real relationship and never thought about having me, but I was already growing in her belly. I am the youngest of three daughters, all having different fathers. My oldest sister's father is in prison and my middle sister's father has been present in her life. As for me, my father left my life when I was two years old. When I was a tad older I gained information that my father was in jail for a rape case. I was young and did not know better, so to me my daddy was just gone. I always wondered will I ever see my father? Why couldn't I grow up with my father? Was I not good enough to get a father?

Dear diary,

Fourth grade year, I discovered my love for dance, that was also the time I met the man who is now my god-father. He was sort of my father figure. He took me places and showed me things only a hood, poor, little ghetto girl can only imagine. Surprisingly this story had darkness behind it. This will be my first time sharing this information, but I want to be completely honest and open with myself and my story that shadows me. My god-father would touch me, but he never tried to penetrate me. I never told people this because this man was essential to my life. He molded me, he taught me, he loved me deeply, and to my family he was my hero. I have always believed in order to be loved, I had to give someone a piece of me. My god-father was free to touch me without fear of being exposed because I needed every other good thing that he brung.

Once I turned twelve my father decided he wanted to pop up. For me it was a bitter sweet moment. I now have this stranger calling

me saying he is my father, but from my knowledge he is a rapist. At least now I can put a voice with a face from a picture I've harbored for years. I never had the audacity to ask him why he went to jail upfront. It was kind of like if you do not know do not mention it. We have spent time together, but in the back of my mind all I can think about is him being a rapist. Then the question of who he raped crossed my mind, really for the first time. At this point I decided that I did not want to gain a relationship with my father, out of anger. In the back of my mind I had some one in my life that cared about me. The anger had me wondering, what man in their right mind would rape someone and leave a daughter searching for their presence?

Diary,

I fell in love for the first time seventh grade year. This boy was so gentle, such a gentleman, so loving. I knew that he was going to be my husband. I lost my virginity to him the summer before eighth grade year. He did not pressure me, and I was not pressured by anyone. I did it because I loved him. I never felt so loved and nurtured before, but he left town and I never heard from him again. When he left he took what I thought was what real love felt like with him. After him it was like I needed to numb this pain I felt. Sex was my go to, sex was my escape from reality. I even got numb to my god-father touching me. If you could love me for those few minutes I would give you something of me, you will not forget about.

Summer before freshman year of high school, I met the person that changed my life completely. I met him at a party. We talked for a month and decided to meet up one day. We had sex in a vacant apartment, rode the bus home, and that was that. Three months later my actions caught up with me. I found out I was pregnant, had two types of STD's, and some sickening truth about the person that was going to be the father of my unborn child. I told my mother I was pregnant on my fifteenth birthday. Then my father found out I

was pregnant through social media, and decided to call me, going off on me. He told me I have no business having sex this early, and I'm going to marry this boy in order to keep the baby. I thought, this son of a bitch, he's completely been absent in my life, had no thought to even apologize for his absence, now has the audacity to tell me how to live my life. At this point this bastard had me fucked up. From that day forward, I told myself there was no way I was allowing this man in my life. I decided to keep my child. After having my daughter, I knew she was going to be a daddyless daughter. Her father comes in and out of her life when it is convenient for him. I finished high school and began college with her by my side.

Dear diary,

Summer before my sophomore year of college, I was in the car with my oldest sister. I had begun to have more and more concerns about who was the missing victim behind my father's imprisonment. I could also see something in my sister's eyes that told me she knew something. It turns out, she knew more than I wanted. She told me the missing piece to this puzzle. She was the girl my father raped. When I was younger I always had a dream about laying in the bed next to my sister, and these sexual images would pop up. I could never imagine my father raping my sister, but he did, and he left. I had so many questions for my family. Why was this such a secret? Why hasn't my mother sat down with me to tell me? It was like she did not understand the importance of my father. I sought the truth out of my mother and father to find closure on this and move on with my life.

I want men out there to understand the importance of a father role in a child's life. The mother is there to teach, love, and nurture, but the father is there to give identity. That is a fundamental building block growing up. It makes life a little hard to go through without, but it is not impossible. I made a vow to myself to do what I had to do to create a life for my child she could cherish and pass down to

her children. I taught myself self-love. I had to put my big girl panties on and make something happen for myself. I had to forgive myself for my actions, in order to grow as a woman. I no longer use being a daddy less daughter as an excuse. I use my testimony as a stepping block to life. I want every daddyless daughter to know that they are not alone and do not let their story hinder them, but push them to be greater than their story.

Mikayla Blevins

My name is Mikayla Blevins, I'm 19 years of age and from Oakland, California. My dad was Vittorio Jackson or "Lil Vic" as they called him. He was an Oakland Native, straight out of Brookfield. He was very caring and did anything for his family, especially for his mother and children, which he had a lot. He had two daughters, including myself and four sons including, one of our step-brothers that he always claimed as his own son. My dad has always been there for me; whenever I needed something I had it. Whenever I wanted something, I had it. The same goes for all his children, we all were set. He made sure he took care of his responsibilities. I remember always going to my grandma's house and running to my dad. I only felt safe around my dad when I was at my grandma house. I was always up under him. We had a tight bond. Even though my mom and dad were not in an intimate relationship they were still best friends until the day he died. I was never comfortable with having a step-father. I personally respect all men that have tried to be a father figure in my life, but I have never called them "dad" because they aren't my dad. The first few months of not having my dad I honestly do not remember. It's like a traumatic experience that you try to forget and actually end up forgetting. I lost weight and I didn't even notice. My sister told me my hair was falling out. I went from having all A's to failing classes and not even caring. I wanted to be rebellious. I wanted people to know that even though I did not have my father there to protect me, I still couldn't be messed with. I did not even want or think about being in a relationship with a guy. My dad taught me how I should be treated and I was scared to give myself away and get treated like I did not mean a thing. Honestly, I have tried to find my father's love in a man. I wanted to feel the same way that my dad made me feel. I wanted to be completely happy when being in a relationship that I set high standards, also feeling that no one could replace his love. This has caused me to barely even be in relationships. And giving myself away has not even come up once in my relationships because of my standards.

I am not in a situation to forgive or hate my father because he was murdered.

Here's my story:

"I'm sorry Kayla…but…" that was all she said through her sobs and I already knew what was coming after. I didn't want to hear it. I didn't want to believe it. I was hoping it was just an early April Fools joke. I went back inside the house, not wanting to watch the sunset with her anymore. The white screen door slammed loudly as I ran to my room.

"No! No! No!" I screamed from the top of my lungs.

It was Easter Sunday and I woke up at the crack of dawn to be early for church. We all got dressed and ate breakfast, ready to leave the house around 9 am. When I first woke up something did not feel right, but I brushed off the weird feeling and continued with my day. At this time my friends did not make it to the early service so I was sitting alone in the choir with all of the adults. That indescribable, weird feeling came back once more but it was short lived since we had another song selection coming up. When I saw my friends coming through the door I felt relieved to no longer be alone.

During our last song I stopped singing. My heart began racing as if I had just run a mile. My short sleeve, sheer top exposed the chills that started to appear on my arms. I stared blankly into the distance, feeling something bad has happened. It was almost like deja vu or like Raven from *That's So Raven* having another vision. I pictured a car pulling up to a parking lot and speeding away, leaving a lifeless body and an empty parking lot. I couldn't tell if my mind was trying to tell me something or it was just wondering about.

About 30 minutes after I received the phone call, my phone blew up with calls from family members saying, "Kayla I love you" or "I'm so sorry." My response was repeated no's through each and every phone call as it felt more real and that this was not just a weird feeling.

We got out of the limousine and walked through the tall brown

church doors, peering at everyone sitting down and staring back at us. The three front rows were reserved for family so we all sat there wearing his favorite color, red. My sister put my letter that I wrote to him in his casket. Sad music began playing and I just sat there as tears filled my eyes. I looked down at my white jeans thinking, "Could this be over already?"

It was now time to bury the body. My cousins were trying to confront me with smiles, hugging me and even holding my hand as we walked over to say our last goodbyes. I looked around at everyone then I stopped and stared at one of my sisters who was only four. She had no idea what was going on right then. How do I tell her that our father was gone forever and never coming back? How do I tell her that this was her very last time seeing him? How do I tell her that she'll never hear his voice again? That lump that forms in your throats telling you to cry came back as they slowly put his casket in the ground.

After the funeral I couldn't help but think, "Now what? What am I supposed to do? How am I supposed to live when he took my heart with him? How am I supposed to move on? When I stepped out into the world could they see a 13-year-old girl without a father? When I go back to school how do I tell my friends that I was away because my dad was a victim of gun violence and sadly did not make it?"

Diary,

A week had passed and I was off to school. I have six brothers but the thought of "Who's going to protect me?" constantly came to mind. The sense of loneliness was strong. I had to see the school's counselor until the end of high school. There were many sleepless nights. For months I did not want to talk about it, let alone talk at all. I had lost all purpose in life. I went from a 4.0 student to not even doing my homework because I wanted to quit. What was the

point if my dad couldn't see me succeed in life?

Diary,

Now that I am older I feel like I have healed. It still hurts to talk about it and I still avoid the topic at times. I feel as though it is very important for a man to be in his daughter life because everyone needs the love and affection from their mother and father. A man should be in his daughter's life because there are going to be times where she is going to need him more than ever. I wish I could tell my father I love him one last time.

Being a daddy-less daughter has taught me to present myself in a lady-like fashion and not all out there in the streets doing things with guys and blaming my father not being in my life for it. Sometimes I look around at other females with dads and I wish they'd appreciate having a dad because I miss mine so much. Not a day goes by that I do not think of him. If I could turn back time I would and spend every day with him. Dad, I know youre watching from above and I just want to say I love you and I'm still going to try to make you proud like I said I would. Love always, your daughter Mikayla.

Arien

My name is Arien and I'm currently a twenty-two-year-old student-athlete from Dallas, Texas. Twenty-two years later and I do not know my father.

Diary, what is it that you do not know about me?

My biological mother has a total of four children with four baby daddies and I am the only one of her kids who does not know their father. Honestly, I knew early on that I wasn't going to have my father growing up and I did not like that one bit. I'm not sure exactly what type of relationship my mother and father had but it couldn't have been too good. Then again, my mother had her own personal battle with drugs so that ruined a lot of her relationships. I have always had a close relationship with her, regardless of her drug addiction. This relationship remained close even after I was taken away from her by the state. My father not being around did not make me feel any type of way about her at the time because I never knew him. It's hard to miss someone you don't even know. At the same time, I'm convinced that his absence drove me and my mother closer. Most of the time, while my siblings would be visiting their dads, I would stay home and spend more time with my mom.

After being in foster care for a little while I was eventually adopted by one of my mom's closest friends growing up, which has been such a blessing. However, this still didn't give me a "father-figure" or "step-father," because my new mom was lesbian. Before and after the adoption my biological mother would have boyfriends that would consider themselves my "step-dad," but I didn't pay them any attention. Not because of them or anything they did; it was more so because I had learned to live without a father-figure. There was one guy that I can honestly say stepped up to the plate for me. My biological mother was with him for quite some time and he happens to be my younger brother's father. He is the closest thing I

have had to a father. We still communicate today although he and my mother have been separated for a year. Also, I cannot forget about the number of my male coaches, uncles, and friend's dads that have always been there as father figures for me throughout everything. At the end of the day, that never made up for my own father not being around.

It is 8:43, we just finished dinner:
Diary,
I was thinking about what I wrote yesterday and it made me think about the moments that embarrassed me inside the most.
I have always been very active in different organizations growing up, like cheer, track, and dance. As I got older I began noticing how many of my friend's and teammate's fathers would be at these competitions and I began to grow jealous of some their relationships. Worst feeling ever. Like, I loved my friends but there were times that I did not want to be around them because I didn't want to watch something so beautiful that I didn't have myself. I never really acted out because of the situation though, I just kept my feelings to myself. However, as I got older I realized that this was afflicting me in a negative way. It messed me up, especially as a teen. As far as relationships go, I learned the "game" from watching my family. I watched how the women acted and how the men acted. Being a daddy-less daughter made me so vulnerable when it came to relationships with guys because I would almost allow anything. They said and could do whatever they wanted and in my eyes that was okay. I was comfortable but that doesn't mean they were treating me right. Nowadays, as far as sex goes, I have standards when it comes to men, both friends and potential boyfriends. It's a must being a daddy less daughter; otherwise, you will go with whatever because you think it feels right. Vulnerability makes itself known in these predicaments. There are a lot of reasons I believe my childhood was stolen from me and being without a father is definitely one. Honestly, at this point I don't care to address the

situation because I don't even know who to blame, him or my mother? I have been successful at the end of the day and I'm still reaching for the stars so I'm fine without him. Mentally, it will still take time to heal because being a daddy-less daughter is just a piece of my story. One thing that has been helping me cope along the way is making sure that all of my guy friends who end up with children are there for them regardless of the relationship with the mother. It is very important that men are there for their daughters. Daughters need their fathers. There is no other way to put it.

If I could tell my father anything it would just be that I love him and I wish he could've been around to watch me blossom. I'm almost sure he would be proud to call me his daughter. I'm reaching the age where we start thinking about marriage and families, and goodness it's so scary for me! I just want to make sure that I marry the right man for my children and I trust that I pick a great guy to be their father and to love all of us unconditionally.

Being a daddy-less daughter has taught me so much but the biggest is being how strong women really are and can be. I grew up without that male protector but both of my mother's instilled strength in me. Strength that no one can take away from me, not even a male. After all of this, even though I am a daddy-less daughter, I still consider myself a success.

DaTionna Kerr

23-year-old student from Kansas City, Missouri.

Dear diary,
I'm not supposed to say this aloud so I'm telling you.

You ever wished someone was dead?
That's how I feel about my so-called "father."
I wish I could erase his name, his memory, what little there is, his voice, and his lies from my life, for good.
Bury him deep in the dirt so he can't bring anyone else any hurt, anymore.
I know there's girls out there who don't have their fathers in their life because maybe he died or they never met him in the flesh. I wish I could trade places with those girls, after reading my story maybe you will understand where I am coming from. Understand the pain I feel from this man's absence; understand the loneliness; understand the devastation he has caused to my mind and to my relationships; understand why I wish him a death sentence.
My dad is David Kerr; really, he is not my dad, only a sperm donor, a giver of last names and unfamiliar grandparents. I never knew David to have a relationship with his parents. I know my grandpa has been in jail since my dad was 14 years old, serving a life sentence. I've never met my grandpa so I don't know why I call him grandpa. He's really just the sperm donor to the sperm donor to me, a stranger. I've never met my 'grandma' in person either but we talk on the phone sometimes. I don't like talking to her because I feel like she's a liar and she claims she took care of me and I don't see how that's possible when I never lived in the same state as her and I would remember if somebody took care of me during the ages she lies about. I feel like everybody on my dad's side is blind to his deadbeat ways, maybe even mental and needs to be evaluated to try to justify him turning his back on his responsibilities.
My my mom and dad met in the mid-90s. I never knew of my mom

to have a relationship with of any kind with him, except in the form of making me. From what my mom said I was three years old when he was charged with what we thought was his final drug case in 1998 and was sentenced to 11 years. And he became the father parenting behind bars, which was no different than when he was out.

I remember when I was in 5th grade we went to Kansas City for winter break. I was living in Maryland at the time. During winter break I remember my aunt took me, my two sisters and brother to visit our dad at the prison. I was young so, of course, I still loved his dumb self. When I was young he would send birthday cards and toys and bears for Christmas through the prison program and it kind of held me in his grip of false fatherhood. That grip lasted for much of my adolescence. Everything was fine up until my freshman year in high school when he was released from jail for a short period. It's winter break, 2009. My sister, DaShonna and I went back to Kansas City because in our heads we were like, 'He's out of jail. We're going to have our "dad" in our life.'

But I was couldn't have been more wrong! When we got to Kansas City our dad came and picked us up from the airport. Everything was all good. He seemed happy, content and ready to embrace his duties as a father and make up for lost tme. After we left the airport we went to our cousins and aunts house, said our "hellos" and "I miss yous," ate, then left. After that we went back to our cousin, Titi's house, which is where we stayed during the break because our dad didn't have his own place yet. Everything went well until he made me upset about. He yelled at me for not picking up some candy wrappers quick enough, even though I always picked up after myself, and other people too for that matter.

The next day my dad made breakfast and I was still upset so I didn't want to eat.

"Oh, you not gone eat?" he asked me before he punched me in my arm. Instead of crying, I punched him back. In my head, I didn't

view him as a "father," only a dad because he wasn't there so until he earned the right he shouldn't be putting his hands on me. He tried to punish me afterwards, by having me wait in the room, but it didn't come off as a punishment since the fight made me so mad that I didn't want to be in his presence.

I called my mom and told her what happened and she gave me his parole officer number. After that he didn't harass me the remainder of the trip. After I got off the phone with my mom I called my dad's girlfriend to come get me and I went to her house for the rest of the day. A few days later we went back home and that's around the time social media was beginning to get the kind of populariy that it has now. By then I had animosity towards him because the whole situation during winter break. For whatever reason my dad and I got into on Facebook of all places!

I don't even remember what the argument was about I just remember him saying, "That's why you're not my daughter, you black dog."

The words stung my soul for a moment and left me so shocked that I couldn't respond anymore. My bestfriend was mad. She started going off on him and it turned into a big mess between them two as well. But maybe a week or two later he ended up going back to jail for drug charges. I was pretty pleased with that.

Once my dad went back to jail I went more than a year before I talked to him again. I never forgave him for hitting me nor for what he said. I just try to get over it and move on. After that Facebook incident I felt like I didn't have to respect him anymore because like he said, *I'm not his daughter.*

For some reason I responded to one of his prison letters. That led us to talk every once in a while, by letter or phone; other times we would email. The federal prison system has a program called Corrilinks, where you can email your loved ones on the Corrilinks website. He did three years in federal prison. He got out again in July 2013, a month after I graduated high school and joined the

Army National Guard. Our conversations were always brief because I always felt like we didn't have nothing to talk about. I didn't know him and he didn't know me.

With my dad not being there, I grew closer to my mom. I realized it's not her fault that my dad got himself in this situation. I used to blame her, secretly, selfishly. Every time I would get into with my dad he would try to down talk my mom. When I was younger I bought into his game but as I grew older his belittling of her made us connect more. Once I realized that it was her who's been there for the entire 23 years and not him his words lost its flame. I do not play when it comes to my mom, so I always felt like I had to take up for her. When I would tell my mom about the stuff he said, my mom would say, "Nana you don't have to take up for me."

I stopped taking up for her maybe four months ago. I just simply stopped talking to him.

Sept. 12th

Tuesday night,

Today in class we discussed single-parent households and the effect it has on kids. Some of the questions we covered/that I answered are as follows:

How has growing up without a father in the household influenced the way you view men/relationships?

Being a daddy-less daughter somewhat has an impact on the guys I choose to deal with. I am very selective when it comes to guys. I do not want anyone that could possibly remind me of him. I've seen my dad mess with four, sometimes more women at a time so I just can't trust it. Play or get played! My standards are very high when it comes to choosing somebody I let into my life. My standards are the reason I have never had a real "boyfriend." I do have the best guy friends ever that I met at Prairie View. I can talk to them about everything. Being a daddy-less daughter can never affect my relationship with my three on campus brothers. They made me realize we do not have to be related to have someone to talk to and

support your dreams.

Did growing up with your father damage or steal your childhood?
I didn't answer aloud, but gave it considerable thought.

My childhood was not stolen from me because I still did things kids do. In my eyes, being an adult not having a dad is worse. I am not in the process of forgiving my dad and I never will. I have no intentions of ever talking to that man ever again in life. In March 2017, my big sister and I got into an argument so I turned her phone off because I pay the bill and she told our dad, mind you he is in jail. He messaged me saying that my sister doesn't need me and I'm not her mother. So of course, I got upset and I told him I don't have any kids so I don't have to do nothing for nobody. After that I texted my sister: *Don't call me when you're hungry, when you need an uber, when you need money. Call your dad because he took care of you all this time, not mom.* Of course, she came apologizing and saying ignore our dad. So, I realized I'm either going to stop talking to my dad or stop talking to my sister. I clearly stopped talking to him. I am not coping with my daddy-less issues. I tried counseling on campus but my issues are deeper than words can explain.

Dear Diary,

Funny, not having a dad in my life has had no influence on my perspective of having kids. I want two kids, but I want to be married beforehand. My future kids will know what a father is and supposed to do. I have no fear of having a daughter because my daughter will be a mini version of me, independent and not dependent on anyone, female or male. *Being a daddy-less daughter taught me to never be dependent on any man and never expect too much. When you expect too much you only end up hurt.*

Mialanni Camp

19 years old from San Antonio, Texas.

Diary,

Stop looking at me like that. I'm not talking. Okay, I will tell you, but I won't reveal to you the entire story.

My father was in my life for a little while and as far as I know his father was always in his life. He was also, and still is, close to his mother. Therefore, the cycle starts with him, not before him.

When I first realized that he wasn't going to be a part of my life I was in middle school. When I was younger he was in the navy, so he was always gone and when he came back he and my mom shared a room and everything so in my mind they were together and happy. There was no fighting or anything that I was ever aware of or that I saw. Now they don't communicate unless it is about me and my twin sister. I've always had a strong relationship with my mother so I think it only made our relationship stronger because a lot of times she is all I have because my dad isn't there. My mother never remarried so I don't have a step-father. However, I consider my uncle to be a really big part of me growing up because he took my sister and I to father daughter dances and things like that and I am very thankful for him being there because I never felt extremely left out.

Psychologically I think that if anything, I had to really convince myself that it wasn't my fault and there is nothing wrong with me. I really didn't act out mostly because my momma does not play those games! I do remember one time we were eating dinner and my mom was on the phone with my dad and he was not cooperating with whatever it was that he needed to do to be able to help take care of us and I went upstairs and wrote a simple email to him saying I hate you. And by the time I got back downstairs my mom was off the phone but not even five minutes later he called back and told my mom what happened.

I don't really do the dating seen much simply because I'm really just trying to do a lot of self-love before I get into a relationship. However, I definitely have standards and sometimes my friends are always saying "you're too picky" and I always tell them I'm not picky but I know what I deserve, what I want and I've seen a good relationship gone bad and that is not what I want for myself. I don't allow anyone to mistreat me be it a man or a woman and I don't go looking for love in a man because I love myself and my family and friends love me and that's enough. I'm really blessed to be surrounded with so many wonderful and loving people.

Having an absent father only affected my childhood to a certain extent. For the most part I got to do everything I ever wanted to do and more. There were some days when my mom was just like "ok, we can't do this right now," but I had no reason to complain because she worked extremely hard to make sure that I was able to do everything I wanted to do and more and then it was always "times two" because I'm a twin. My father not being there really made my childhood even more fun, as crazy as that sounds, because my mom was always doing something with us and spending time with us.

I always feel like I am in the process of forgiving my father. It seems like once I make peace with something he does something else that I have to make peace with. For example, I hadn't talked to my father in about six or seven years and then my freshman year of college I'll never forget how dumbfounded I was when his name popped up on my phone on a Monday night in November. At first, I really wasn't going to answer but I knew if I didn't I would regret so I did. At first it was very awkward being that I was practically talking to a stranger but, after a little while that seemed like forever it was a comfortable conversation and kind of explained why he hadn't been calling and said he was sorry. After that he called every so often and even sent a little spending cash which was appreciated. Fast forward to spring break, I was home for break but he failed to

mention that he would be in my hometown at the same time I was. I was really upset when I found out but it didn't hurt much because it was like it was kind of expected at this point. I really don't talk much at all about my dad. It's just not something that I dwell on and I don't feel like it is something that I want to focus on. So I simply say a prayer for my father and I just hope he gets it together for himself. For myself, I always remind myself how loved I am and how much God loves me because I don't have my biological father but I have a heavenly father that can do more for me than anyone ever could.

To the "man" that chooses not to be in his daughter's life, I really hope you change your mind because she needs you more than you'll ever know. She is going to grow up in to this beautiful lady and it will tear you a part knowing you had nothing to do with it and everything at the same time. See you weren't there physically, but you were on her mind constantly. She used you to stoke the fire under her to succeed and be something in spite of anything she went through because you were not there. If my father was in my life I would tell him thank you for not leaving me. For helping succeed in my life and for loving me unconditionally and for supporting all of my dreams.

Diary,
What have I taken away from this experience?

Being a daddy-less daughter has taught me a lot. The main thing is to be able to forgive. That's one thing my dad has taught me as well as to know my worth. I used to hate it when sometimes my mom would just get really fed up and say something like, "he is just no good." I would find myself trying to defend him and I didn't realize that she was only saying and doing things to protect me.

Not being around my dad had a spiritual and emotional impact because I went through a lot with my family and I know sometimes I had to question God like why me, and why my family? I definitely

feel like my life would be better with my dad in because my family wouldn't have to struggle so much and it's always nice to have both parents. Sometimes, it's just the little things that matter the most, like having your dad threaten to beat up your boyfriend or take you on daddy-daughter dates.

I'm pretty sure he does not know the full effect that he has had on me by walking out and I don't know if he takes full responsibility. I do know that my dad loves me regardless of what has happened. I know a lot of his recent actions don't show it, but I choose to remember the good times I had with my dad.

Alanna

February 1,

My father showed up to my graduation late, missing me walk across the stage for my diploma, but I still smiled when I saw him sitting in the audience.

February 2,

When I was younger we had a normal father daughter relationship until Valentine's day of 2009, when he left. My mom left the house and business to get away from their toxic marriage. They soon got a divorce and ever since then he hasn't been an active, reliable father. Years passed and I was still holding on to hope that he'd someday reenter his three-daughter's life, but hope soon vanished when he did not attend anything of our events, call to check up on us, send monetary or loving support. My mother and father had a rollercoaster relationship, before the divorce. I remembered when I was younger my parents arguing at night, physically and verbally. There would be nights I would hear yelling, slamming of doors and sounds of physical altercations. Their shaky relationship did not really affect my relationship with my mom until the divorce occurred. I did not know who to blame so I blamed her for a long time. I thought there was no reason she left behind our lives and not wanting us to see our dad or that he did not make it a point to see or call us.

My mother has her father in her life, so it was hard for her to connect with us and for us to come to her because she wouldn't understand what we were going through. I remember when we were packing I told my grandparents that my mom doesn't know how we feel, because she has her dad, our papa. My father didn't walk out on us, my mom left him. We packed up and left our house, business, friends and memories. He did not walk out on us, but he never came to us after we left.

February 5,

My papa, Willie Walker, has been there through it all for my sisters and me. What my father didn't do, my papa did. What my father did not go my papa did. He has attended my orchestra concerts, ceremonies, homecoming, prom, graduation, move in day for college, all while my father was nowhere to be seen. I've seen him treat my nana like a queen and my mama and auntie like princesses.

February 6,

Having an absent father is tough, especially when you go to school and all your classmates have active fathers. When we had to fill out papers at school, do school projects or have father breakfast, I was embarrassed because I didn't have my father's number to put down in the space. In grade school I remember my school had father and daughter breakfast and my papa came instead of my father. It was normal to me, but when kids would ask if that's was my dad I got embarrassed and told them he was my papa and lied about where my dad was. Or when my friends would talk about their dads or I had to watch them get picked up by their dad, I would make up a lie again. It hurts even more because my sisters are younger than I am, so they were much younger when the divorced happened which caused them to know less and have less quality time with our dad. Throughout grade school I continued to lie about where my dad was and who he was. He has been a FBI agent, a manager for famous people or in the Navy, or lives in New York City, or California with another family, that's why he never visits us much. After the divorce, 4th-8th grade was rough. I was a rebellious child. My behavior in school and home took a left turn. It got so bad that I'm certain my mom's number was on speed dial on some of my teacher's phones. I was very intelligent but I had serious behavioral issues. I am the oldest in the house, so I knew my little sisters looked up to me, and I knew I wasn't being the best role model but at that time I didn't care. I was angry at everything and everyone.

February 10,

When I was younger I was molested by two family friends. One of them was close to my family. My mother and father found out about him, but the other man no one knows about. The one that my parents found out about I do not remember when he first touched me or how it happened. I was so young I didn't think it was normal nor weird. I was just oblivious to the entire situation. I didn't find the need to tell my parents. He and his family lived with us, so the events occurred about daily. It went on for a couple of years without anyone finding out. I can replay the day repeatedly when my parents found out. My dad and mom went crazy on the guy, but my mom was mad at me. I was much older when they found out, so I think she thought I was being "fast" because they did not know how long it had been happening. There were no charges pressed. His mother, which I consider my second mom and her daughters my sisters till this day, were shocked. We all just put that to past and silently vowed not to speak on it.

The second time I was molested was scary. I felt alone since I didn't know who to tell. It was soon after my parents found out about the other one, so I was scared to tell them. Being a "victim" to those acts I get these reoccurring sharp pains in my pelvic region. I buried all this; however it still haunts me in my life with relationships, my mental and self-esteem.

February 16,

My parents met in high school and became high school sweethearts. They stayed together even after going to separate colleges in different states. My mom was around 31 when the divorce happened. She never really had a boyfriend other than him, so after the divorce her pick of men wasn't too great. She has been involved in toxic mental, spiritual, emotional and physically abusive relationships. I didn't realize that it has influenced my life

negatively, it has affected me in my relationships and my thoughts on men. I am strong I know that for a fact, however, when it comes to guys, relationships or sex I am weak, and I know they can sense that giving them the opportunity to abuse it. It took me until September of 2017 to realize that I have a fear of abandonment and trust issues. I was so quick to find love and fill in the void I had that I started to settle for less and please them. I loved the "bad boy" vibe because it gave me a rush of excitement. I'm 19 and I've been in some mentally and physically abusive relationships, thinking it was love when in fact it was more of a strong like or lust.

February 18,

When I was 16, I talked to this guy who was new to the school. He was very handsome but a bad boy. My friends told me that he wasn't the one and that he'll cause a lot of heartache. I didn't listen. We were only together for one month and it was an abusive relationship. He would never hit me with his balled fist. There was only pushing and pullin, along with verbal and emotionally abuse. I got grounded and wasn't allowed to see him, so he started cheating on me. I distinctly remember him saying, "What was I supposed to do, wait on you?" That broke me. After that my close friend was there for me and we got together. We dated for two years. It was a regular high school relationship. I ended it because I was graduating and attending college. Losing my best friend and my boyfriend right before prom and graduation was hard. I was emotionally unstable. That last semester of high school was tough, I gained a lot of wait, I stressed ate, I looked at myself differently, my self-esteem was low. As a result, I spent my summer working two jobs and working on myself and getting closer to God in order to be a better me before going into college. Thankfully I came in to college so happy and so peaceful. It was going all great until I crossed paths with an old classmate from high school and everything went south. From September to October of 2017 I didn't know who I was. When we

started talking everything was so wonderful. He was everything I could have asked for. Opening doors, calling me all this sweet stuff, taking me out on dates, telling me beautiful things. There was a lot of red flags that I overlooked and just believed everything he was telling me. He was what we call all talk with no action. I found myself putting myself last by always being on his time and setting my business and duties aside to be with him. I was just excited to have found somebody after a terrible break up months prior. Knowing this guy had a baby on the way by his ex, I didn't let that run me off. I went through the "baby mama drama" with him. Things started to go left, the same day I had to tell him some news is the same day he ended our little relationship. After that I didn't want to tell him the news, but I knew I soon had to. I had a pregnancy scare, and I was so scared and didn't know what to do because he already had a child on the way and I was a freshman in college not wanting to have a child anytime soon. Prayerfully with God's grace I wasn't pregnant.

February 21,

The most important thing us females need is to love ourselves first; I always say, "Self-love is priceless." Being a daddy-less daughter is tough but we as queens must keep fighting and believing that better is coming and we will soon overcome the hurt and take back control of our lives. By stop blaming others and take control with God's help is a must. An amazing author, speaker, minister and teacher, Jotina Buck, said in her book, *Change your language, Change your life,* "Define your values and be authentic to yourself. Remind yourself that you were created in greatness; you are exceptional, and you are precious in God's eyes." I must remember that I am fearfully and wonderfully made and possess faith to accept and face my past so that my healing can start.

I did my thing despite being fatherless and despite all the mistakes I made. I graduated high school with a 3.7 GPA and 12 college

credits, put on the First Annual Black Heritage Program in Tomball ISD, resulting in my being featured in the African American News and Newspaper. I am also in the process of founding a non-profit organization. With the support of my mother and grandparents I have been blessed to be able to attend the HBCU in Texas, Prairie View A&M University, as a political science major and a minor in animal science. I am a work in progress, I am a success story and my story is not done; it's only the beginning.

This is to Stanley "Leo" Gaskin:

Thank you, daddy, thank you for being there and the next minute you're gone. Thank you for giving me heartache and pain, with that you have made me stronger and eager to want and do better. You and my past won't dictate my future. Wherever you are I pray and hope you are doing okay and that God has angels surrounding you. I love you and I miss you.

Natalia (from *The Women of Sugar Hill*)

Dear Diary: *Summer, 1992*

Daddy never said much to me; I only seen him in the streets when me and my brother, KJ, used to go to the corner store for the family or when we went to steal something to eat. We usually went together, even though I think KJ hated me. He told me he did once.

Sometimes I went alone.

Sometimes I passed by daddy. Sometimes he would speak and keep going.

Sometimes he would pass right by me without a word if he was with another woman.

One day he walked with me to the store and bought me a Snicker, a big bag of Doritos, and a Dr. Pepper.

"Hey Tally," he said.

"Hey pops." He caught me off guard. He was standing on the corner.

"Where you headed?"

"The store."

"Got any money?" he asked.

"No."

He looked around before saying, "Wanna come to my house for an hour or two?" His eyes were red.

"Yea," I said, curious because I'd never been to his house.

We went to the store without saying much else to each other except he asked about school once. I lied about making the A-B honor roll.

Even though daddy was buying, I stole a pack of Now & Later before we left the store for later on. The sun had sweat pouring from daddy's head that he didn't bother to wipe away.

"That blow pop good?" he asked because I was making slurping noises.

"Mhmm," I managed in between slurps.

Daddy smiled and then was quiet again until we reached his house. He kept fidgeting with a piece of broken car antenna that he had in his pockets, like I saw crackheads carry. I didn't know if my daddy was a crackhead or not but where he took me was definitely a crackhouse. Mama said he wasn't but she'd say anything in his defense because she was still in love with him.

There wasn't no other children at daddy's house. It was hot because of the weather and the fans could only blow hot air. It wasn't fully furnished, a couch, a table, and a couple of broken chairs. A female and two men sat in a corner looking lost and dirty.

I can't ever forget the house. It was a pathetic looking place, brown and white like half of the houses in Sugar Hill. But it did have all of its windows.

I was kind of nervous. No one spoke when we walked in. I stood by the door playing with another blow pop until daddy broke the silence. He was still fidgeting with that antenna.

"Will you do daddy a favor?"

It shook me a little hearing his voice inside the house. I guess I loved my daddy and missed him. I wanted to please him. Maybe he would come back home.

"Yes sir," I said.

"To the couch," he said to the adults there. The two men and woman moved over to the couch. "I told ya I would get some money."

"That ain't money," the woman said. She was daddy's girlfriend. Name was Toya. She stared me up and down. "Hell, might be better than money."

Daddy bent down and held me by the arms. "Now what I need for you to do for me Tally is play a game. You like games don't you?" I shook my head yes. "These two here gonna play Santa Claus and you pretend it's Christmas. You can do that right?"

"Yes sir." Daddy must've remembered how much I liked Christmas presents.

"You sit on their lap and tell them what you want. Does that sound good?"

"Yea. I mean yes sir" I was kind of excited and a little bit scared because they didn't look too clean. I wanted to say it but I couldn't because of daddy's red eyes.

Daddy patted me on the head and said, "Don't be scared and be nice to them."

I shook my head and put my blow pop back in the bag.

They gave daddy a small bag of something and he went into the bathroom with the lady.

The first man, named Jake, sat on the arm of the couch. He spoke to me first.

"How are you doin' little pretty lady?"

"Okay, I guess."

"Come tell Santa what you want for Christmas." He sounded scary.

Pretending, I managed after sitting in his lap., "Santa, I been good all year. Can you get me a bike out your bag and bring it my house on Christmas Eve?"

"Let me see." He reached into a plastic bag and fumbled around and pulled out a piece of paper with something written on it. Then he said, "Don't seem like you been too nice this year, not according to my elfs?"

"They some lyin' son-of-a-bitches," I said.

The other man laughed. Jake grabbed me by the waist and bounced me on his lap some.

"Ain't nothin' we can't fix so we can get you that bike."

"Thanks, Santa."

"Now be quiet while I see what we can do to fix your list." His hand started running across my back, then to my stomach.

Charles, the other man, interrupted. "Say man, when you gone let me get my chance."

"I ain't done yet," Jake said.

man, we done." Charles had gone back into a corner. Daddy came back out.

"Want some ice cream?" he asked.

"Yes sir."

He handed me my bag and said he'll see me later on. I cried at his gate really quickly and then fixed my face before somebody saw me. In Sugar Hill, you gotta be tough.

I never got that ice cream but I knew I had made daddy proud of me. If I keep doing him favors he'll come back home and love us again.

Daisha Curry

Hello, my name is Daisha Curry, I am a 19-year-old girl from a small city, Waco, TX. My mother had me at the age of 17, which made things harder on her being a single parent. In my 19 years of living I've never seen my biological fathers face. I am his only daughter next to his other four sons. My brothers were raised by my father but I guess I wasn't lucky enough to be a part of his life.

My first diary entry on this:

Imagine being the middle child and you're the only one who has never seen your dad's face and the only thing you ever received from him was a card with twenty dollars in it. Then imagine your dad's family while they sit back and watch it all happen as if they think it's okay.

My dad has a family full of women. The most shocking thing of it all is knowing his mother, my grandmother, won't even try to email me back. I tried reaching out to my father so many times with no luck that it has gotten to the point I don't even want a relationship anymore. With me being 19 going on 20, what can he possibly teach me now that my mother hasn't? What could he possibly do to benefit me in any way other than give me money?

Watching my brothers and sister get the attention from their fathers that I never felt before was a heart-wrenching feeling because I didn't ask to be here, I didn't ask for him to abandon me like I was a dead weight on his shoulder. My big brother's dad was the closest thing I ever had to a father figure. Christmas time was the best time. He treated me like I was his own, until I got older, then he didn't. It took me years to finally understand I did not need him or my real dad. It took me years to finally say, "Daisha, why are you still crying about this?"

I lost my virginity at 14. I don't blame anyone for my mistakes of being fast but one thing I wish I had was guidance from a father's

point of view. I went from relationship to relationship seeking comfort feeling. My mother did a wonderful job raising me but that empty void is not a feeling one parent can take away. At 16, I got my first job at IHOP as a server. I worked myself to death just so I could provide myself with the things my mom could not. I felt that she had other things to take care of other than paying for me some new clothes, shoes and makeup. She had two other children to take care of as well. By the age of 17 I bought my first car. I was set on being this independent woman and getting everything on my own. Naturally, when you buy a used car, things go wrong and I had to immediately get another one. I did not want to go back to asking my mother for rides so I kept working to stack up some bread for a better car while trying stay in track in high school, which was the hardest thing I had to do. Because my mom had so much on her plate I became focused on finding a sugar daddy and thinking about that now just makes me so mad because as teenager, life should be nothing but fun. You shouldn't have to stress while your father is laid up doing lord knows what.

I feel my childhood was stolen from me because the absence of my father. While all my friends went out partying or to a big event, I was out grinding for things I needed and material things I seen everyone else have. I hated the fact that my brother, my cousins and everyone else I knew were handed everything. It seems like a petty thing but imagine you having this hurt going on and then you have to pick up slack from not having that second parent. What hurt me to the core was being drugged by a family member thinking they'll never do something like that to me over money.

Being a daddy-less daughter only made me the woman I am today. Yeah, I wish I had that backbone but looking back on it, it was all a lesson. I don't believe in coincidences. Because he wasn't in my life means he was not meant to be in my life. I probably wouldn't be as strong as I am today.

I've already forgiven my father for his absences. Right now, I am in

college making something of myself. My mom didn't have to force me to come here or talk me into it. I want the best for myself. I can't hold a grudge over someone I never met before. I can't blame my mother for his absence. She did the best she could by working long shifts to provide for the kids she made and raised. She is the true definition of an independent woman, and I salute her for that

The best advice I could give to a father to be or someone that's already a father is, it doesn't matter how old they are, your child needs you, your child needs a father. A mother can only do so much providing and raising. She didn't make the child on her own so why leave her with all the responsibilities as if she planned it.

I used to cry about it, now I make my pain reflect in my hustle...

Aliah Page

Her Untold Story, a Night of Diary Talking:

Me and my dad used to be close. I would even go as far to claim that I used to be a "Daddy's Girl." Its funny how when you're little that you don't see things for the way they are. When I was younger I put my dad on this high pedestal. In my eyes, he showed me the blueprint of what a man was supposed to look like. But what I failed to realize is my dad hid most of his flaws away from me when I was younger. I came to find out that he and my mother were having relationship issues because he failed time and time again to stay faithful. My mom and dad had a real toxic, on again off again relationship where they argued about any and everything. I really knew something was wrong when they broke up and he moved out of the house into his own apartment.

For a while my dad and my mom had split custody of us. Whenever it was my dad's turn to come pick us up he would always be late which my mom would never let us forget and always had to make a comment about him not caring about us. One day my dad told us that we were going to Six Flags with his "friend." Of course, as kids we didn't think nothing of it and were excited to go. The day we went to Six Flags we met his friend, which was his side chick at the time. Her name was Michelle. She was a curvy Mexican woman and she brought her kids along with her. I didn't understand what was going on at the time but I knew something wasn't right. After the day at Six Flags I asked my mother about the woman my dad brought around us. I didn't know then but apparently that caused problems because my mom and dad were working on getting back together. After my mom found out about this she began being cold towards him and began to speak down on him more and more to us. It felt like it was a war between them, like we, the kids, were being used as weapons between them.

My grandparents on my dad's side decided to not watch us when my mom had to go to work, causing her to pay babysitters and family on my dad's side to watch us. This tension between my mom and dad, lack of support from family, and the toxic relationship between them began to be too much for my mom. She decided she wanted to move back to Louisiana because she would have more support from her family to watch us while she is working. Apparently, my dad agreed that we should go to Louisiana with my mom as long as we were with him on holidays. My mom began to move all our stuff to Louisiana. Then my dad changed his mind and went to court. The court decided that we needed to stay in the state that we were born in. My mom decided to still move to Louisiana since all her things were moved at this point and our dad, now, had main custody of us. After she moved to Louisiana, we stayed with my dad and for the most part everything was still the same. Then he tried to slowly introduce Michelle in our lives. She would still be doing side chick things such as buying things for us, but we would never see her face. For example, she would buy us McDonalds, leave it at the door, then she would knock at the door, and run back to her car before we could see her. There came a point where my dad and Michelle got serious and he decided to bring her around us more. Eventually they moved into a house together, merging with me and my sisters with her son and her daughter. I mean I get what they were trying to do by having the whole "mixed family" thing come together but it never really worked out.

My dad went back to his old ways and started being unfaithful, which brought tension into the house. Michelle's kids really didn't like my dad because they did not appreciate the way he was treating their mom and they didn't like us for the fact that we were his kids and we didn't like them back. My dad and Michelle had an on again off again relationship like him and my mother did. At the time that just seemed normal to me, so I didn't think nothing of it until it seemed like his priorities shifted. My dad began to become selfish,

especially when it came to his finances. Whenever me and my sister would ask him for something it was as if we were burdening him with too much. Then when Michelle would ask him for money and it wasn't a problem. I was not the only one who felt this shift in his priorities. My sisters also felt it and Michelle took advantage of it. She became too comfortable when it came to discipline when my dad was gone to work. She would just do petty things like antagonize us, telling us we eat too much. Every time we were in the kitchen she would always question us and play favoritism between my and my sisters by leaving the house with my two sisters and leaving me at home alone. I would tell my dad all these things she would do to us but he would either brush it off or tell me I was being dramatic. Ever since then I started building resentment towards my dad because I felt that he was ignoring my well-being for his own satisfaction.

A couple of years later he and Michelle broke up for good and my dad got his own house. Several months after he sustained an injury while on the job. He had to get surgery on his arm and back and was out of work for some time. He filed a lawsuit against the company. During this time of waiting, he grew really bitter. He started drinking more, going out at night more and became overly mean to us. He took out his frustrations of not having a job out on us. When he disciplined us he started to cross the line. He would use unnecessary force to get his point across. For instance, I remember he told me to clean the upstairs bathroom. I got the supplies and as I'm walking upstairs he pushed against the stairs, making me fall down the stairs. Then he was just yelling at me the whole time saying that I should have been cleaned the bathroom, how I'm ungrateful I am, and all.

It would just be a constant battle living with him. I began to feel depressed because I felt he didn't care about me. He would only be home during the day and sometimes in the evening and he would go out to drink, party, or whatever at night. The only interaction I

received with my dad was when he would discipline us. I ended up telling my mom how I was very depressed and didn't want to live with him anymore. She had moved to Colorado and I went to stay with her. While there, my dad ended up getting his life together a little bit and got him a new job and a new girlfriend. They became serious enough to move into a house together. I would go visit him occasionally because I did miss him even though I knew he'd developed a drinking problem. Whenever I was at my dad's house I would always feel like I was walking on eggshells because he is a control freak and he wants everything neat and spotless. In my dad's house there were two living rooms, the main living room and the living room in the furnished basement. One evening, I decided to watch TV in the main living room and for some reason he had a problem with it. He told me that I couldn't watch TV in the main living room because it's only for decoration. I called him out because what he was saying didn't make sense. Everyone watched TV in this living room but for some reason on this day he had a problem with me watching TV in the main living room. Honestly, I think he was hungover and the noise from the living room was irritating him. He repeated himself and told me to go to the downstairs living room and I told him no because the downstairs living room doesn't have Netflix, which is what I was watching at the time. He had the nerve to put his hand on my throat and yelled at me to go downstairs. I smacked his hand away from my throat and told him to get his drunk self out my face. He tried to snatch me up again and I swung on him. All the resentment that I'd been feeling for years was finally let out in that moment. And it felt good.

Phyleshia Locke

I just want to say that Phillip Locke is going to be mad if he ever reads this one day, but that's the way it is. My name is Phyleshia Locke I'm 21 years old and I'm from Seattle Washington, but I have been living in Houston, Texas for six years now.

Dear Diary,

I do not know my father. I never met him before. He was never in my life and from what I gather, didn't want to be. If you made me pick him out of a line up I couldn't tell you who he was. I have no idea what his relationship is with his parents or if his father was there for him. My father was embarrassed of me, I think. My mom was only 16 years old and he was older, so I think he didn't want people to know about their relationship and decided to cancel it all together. As a child I never really paid attention to the fact that my father wasn't there. As I got older, like middle school older, it became a problem for me. I had already hit puberty, so I had butt and boobs and boys were looking and talking. During this strange but natural devopment stage, I needed a man to tell me the ins and outs of how boys would act and what they would want out of a girl.

Dear Diary,
I'm back…

The only relationship my parents had was one I can't speak on because I wasn't alive to see it. I know that my father was a drug dealer, so he gave my mom nice things and I'm going to assume their relationship was fine until she got pregnant. As of now I don't think my mother even speaks to my father.

The connection with my mother started at birth, really. She is the only parent that I was nurtured by, so it would only be normal that I flocked to her. We have a strong bond. I'm the mini version of her even though I don't really like to admit it. I'm the oldest child out

of three so I hold myself accountable for a lot of things that happen in my house. I think because my mom knew my dad wasn't in my life she was more active in mines than most moms. Everything I did she was there for, unless she had to work, which was untestable because she was a single parent and had to get it on her own. My mom is a hustler and it makes me respect her because a lot of people's moms wouldn't do what my mom has done in her life and I know that's why we are so close. I pretty much know everything about her.

Growing up my little brothers had their dad for a while. He and my mom got married and they were together. He wasn't a father to me, more of a homeboy in a sense. He did father type things but mentally and physically I didn't feel a fatherly connection. He was fun and treated me like I was his kid. We would go to the hood and play at the park or go to a BBQ, stuff like that. He tried to make it work. I went to family events that his side of the family had so I was treated like I was one of his kids. But something was still missing.

My brother's dad went to jail a lot. We'd been to the county jail, to the prison, then the camps. I had seen it all before I was 13 years old. I used to always get so pissed off because I wanted him to be a complete father to my brothers. They needed it more than I did. I just wanted them to grow up knowing they had a man in their life to look up to. All the time I was so focused on him being a father for them that if he was trying to nurture me and show me affection I ignored it. Give it to them, they need it. This didn't make up for the fact that my father was gone. It made me forget about it for some years. Even though I wasn't really upset, I still wanted to know why the hell I had to be the child left out the picture. It wasn't my fault Phillip slept with my mom and got her pregnant then played a cowardly, lifelong game of hide-n-seek.

Diary,

I've always tried impress a boy/man, not for Phillip, but for myself. I always had the feeling that if I could impress this dude and make him look at me then I'm doing good. I didn't walk around wearing slutty clothes or anything, but I bought clothes that fit just right and made my butt look real nice. It was just my way of feeling good about myself. Parent teacher conferences were annoying to me. When I would see both parents come in with their kid and sit down it made me mad, like damn why can't I have that, so I would always go outside and play because I didn't want to look at the happy families. My message for my behavior was that I needed help! I needed someone to tell me *it's okay to not have a father, you can still do everything that everyone else can. When people look at you they don't see a girl with no father, they see the girl who has potential to do anything she puts her mind to.* This is a big reason I ran track. Running made me feel like I was getting away from it all. I felt if I could just run long enough for the pain to go away I would be fine. I ran because that was the only time in my life when I didn't have to think. I just had to run and run fast. Smoking weed became a big part of my routine. Getting high would just put me in a state of mind that was so relaxing that I didn't need to think either. I could just chill and enjoy the moment I was living in.

Being a daddyless daughter has affected my relationships in many ways. I have taken advantage of a situation, but they didn't really know. I allowed men to have sex with me that I shouldn't have but I didn't have my feelings involved, it was just sex for me. My very first relationship was with this boy named Ben and I thought I was in love and he was in love with me. He took my virginity and our relationship was fine but at some point, things started to change. We still dated for a little while, but he started having feelings for someone else. Had I had a man to tell to watch out for those signs I wouldn't have gotten my heart broken when he broke up with me; I would've knew how to take it. I was mistreated by a man and it was out of line when I was younger. I used to go on RV trips with my

great aunt and uncle and I had 3 cousins. We were all around the same age. It was 2 girls and a boy. Usually, it was always us 4 but this time my boy cousin wanted to bring my other cousin, BJ. We went to sleep, and I can't really feel much when I'm sleep but something in me said wake up. When I woke up BJ had his hands in my pants and was fingering me. I tried to kill him with a knife, but the family wouldn't let me.

Outside of this incident, my childhood was great. I didn't miss out on anything. My mom and grandparents made sure that anything we needed we had it and more. For Christmas my mom would have our house full of gifts and toys and everything a kid dreams of. My dad not being there, he just missed out on me growing up, learning the type of kid I was and what I did and didn't like.

Dear Diary,

I'm coping fine. There comes a time in a person life when you just come to grips with what a situation is and how it's going to be. That doesn't mean it will stay that way, but you have to come to peace. I'm working on praying every day so I can be healed from the situation and remove hate from my heart or aggression toward the situation itself. I joined Daddyless Daughters: Changing My Destiny, Incorporated to help start my healing. I was lost I didn't know how to start healing from the situation to be honest it was something so far in the back of my mind that it would've never came up without this organization to bring it out. A girl's first love is her father period no matter what. By not being in your daughter's life is opening a lot of doors for hurt, abandonment, mistreatment, and pain. By not being in your daughte's life, she doesn't know what to look for in a man. She doesn't know how a man should treat her or if he is treating her correctly. Your daughter needs your love and attention. She needs you to tell her, *No that's wrong. Don't let someone treat you that way.* If you are not there then she will end up just how

you left her mom, with a child who has no father because to her a dad not being there is normal.

Dear Daddy,

I feel like me telling this story will get you to want to connect with me and it shouldn't have taken me calling you out for you to get the point. I just want to know why you thought it would be ok to leave my life and not give an explanation. Tell me why you never thought to speak to me at one of my parades or try to interact with me. I might have been nice and talked to you. Did you know I was one of the best track runners for a long time? Did you know I graduated from high school with no problems? Did you know I was in college and didn't quit and that those little child support checks didn't help pay for any of it. There is a lot you don't know about me and that's your fault because you should've been there, and you weren't so I don't owe you anything but I think you have some explaining to do. I don't really want to have kids I'm so scared that my baby father will not want to be in their life and I can't let them deal with what I went through. It's not fair for any human being to go through this. I mostly fear having a daughter. Women are hard and dangerous people. Being a daddy-less daughter has taught me a lot. I'm in college and I'm working my way through life without a father. It shows how strong I really am and how much I believe in the process. As dadyless daughters, are judged by men, women, and children every day because they think we are going to fail but we prove them wrong every time just by waking up and accomplishing something. Being a daddyless daughter has showed me that I have a lot of fight in me and that I'm held to an even higher standard because I have one piece of the puzzle missing that somebody else doesn't.

You are bigger than not having a father. You can do great things. I promise when people look at you they don't see your hurt and your pain, but I know it's there because me and you are the same.

Some advice that I would give for a daddy-less daughter is build a relationship with God and the reason I say that is because I'm trying to build my relationship with God and as I'm doing that I am becoming more at peace with myself and everything I ever went through. When you need to vent, talk to God or read this story and just let it marinate. God will listen and help you. I don't think my life would've been better had my "Father" been there. His absence made me a stronger woman and independent. I feel like if he would've been there I wouldn't have those traits so strongly so I kind of thank him for not being there. The only thing he would've been good for was teaching me how to find a good man, but then again, maybe not because of who he is. My "Father didn't need to be added to my life. I was put in this situation for a reason.

My father has power over me and he shouldn't. Anytime someone makes you mad or makes you feel out of your norm they have power over you. The way you take that power back is by forgiving them and coming to peace with yourself so that you aren't upset when his name comes up or you're asked a question about it. He also has power over my life because everything he didn't teach me has an effect on me, whether I want to believe it or not. Males are funny things. I don't consider myself naïve to them because as you grow and you learn what hurt is and what pain is, there is nothing a man can do to you that will affect you as much anymore. He will either build up on what has already happened to you or he will break you from what you have already.

I consider myself a success story because for one, a lot of women wouldn't just come out and tell you their story and not be afraid of what someone might think or even say. My life has been a crazy one but every time I accomplish something that adds to my success. Being a daddy-less daughter is a success story in itself. I worked hard to get where I am today in life and I didn't have a father to help me do it. Through all my trials and tribulations, I was able to come to college and meet women just like me who I believe were all

put in my life to make me even more successful. I'm not ashamed of my life and I thank God every day that I can wake up and just be happy. I'm not all the way at peace with myself but I'm getting there and every day is a step further. I thank you for taking the time out to listen to my story and I pray it helps answers some of the questions or concerns you have within yourself about your father not being there. Remember this, it's a permanent hurt but it's only temporary pain; time heals all wounds.

Anonymous

From the Diary of a daddyless daughter:

I know who my father is and he is close with his mom but he is a fatherless son. I realized when I was 12 that he wasn't going to be in my life, the peaking age when I needed him the most. My parents never dated, I was somewhat born out of the open because they had no relationship, just a physical connection. They never got along and still don't. It didn't drive me and my mother's relationship apart but in my early teens it made me more rebellious towards her and my stepfather. I felt like the more rebellious I became the more my dad would have to be in my life.

I had somewhat three father figures step into my life, including my grandfather before his passing in 2007. It never made up for my dad being absent because no matter what, I still craved him. My rebellion led me to guys and also led me to believe I knew a lot. I became a "smart ass," so to speak. Talking back to my mom and stepdad, just being disobedient for no reason was normal for me. Being a daddyless daughter, there have been some rough years since I started dating. From being in abusive relationships to getting continuously cheated on and even getting pregnant at the tender age of 18. I think allowed guys to mistreat me because I always had a weakness to be loved. I never had a standard for guys it was just a "if I like you, I like you" type of thing when I was in high school and beginning of college. With my sexual issues I can say I didn't lose my virginity until my senior year of high school, but once I did it became a drug for me heavily in my first year of college. Sex was a getaway for me to just feel perfect and loved for a temporary moment. But once I realized that you can't "sex" your problems away, it was easier to resist but I still became a little sex addict.

I had a wonderful childhood without my father honestly. He was mostly there in my early years, in and out, but my childhood was awesome because of my mom and grandparents. I forgave him in

2016 because I realized I can't live my life being angry towards him. He's living his best life so why can't I live mine? My dad knows that I never really had a grudge, but I just don't have respect for a man who wanted to abort his child and have a whole new wife and child pretending like his eldest daughter is non-existent. The Bible says forgive to be forgiven, so that's what I did. The way I cope with my daddyless situation would be just numbing the pain in many ways. My advice to fathers who choose to not be in their daughter's life would be why? Why hurt her? She didn't choose to be here. Why just throw the relationship you could have with your daughter away? I never understood that. It's selfish and very inconsiderate.

When I got pregnant my freshman year of college, my child's father told me that he would not be in my child's life if I kept it or not, point blank period. I just think cowards are out here impregnating women and just aren't man enough to handle responsibility. Seriously, if you know you aren't ready to be a father to your daughter or precious son then just practice safe sex or stop getting these women to lay down with you unprotected. Be a man or just stop being sexually active until you are. I wish I could tell my dad that he just needs to get help. Pray for forgiveness, admit his wrongdoings towards me and move forward together. His absence influenced my perspective on having kids because I promised myself I wasn't going to bring no child into this world without a father. My pregnancy took a turn because of my child's father not wanting to be apart of it. Sticking to my selfish promise I had a surgical abortion at 16 weeks. Being that my child's gender was a girl, it's heart wrenching and just makes me feel like history could've been repeated. So I had that fear and still do, just hopefully when I am ready for a child the child's father will be supportive.

Being a daddyless daughter has taught me that my story will never ever be my downfall. My words of encouragement to a girl who has been in my shoes would be stay strong don't let it be the end. I have prospered after so much in my life, from being in college to a

professional DJ and social butterfly. My lack of a relationship with my father impacted me more emotionally because I used to always cry or feel suicidal and try to get his attention by doing the most dramatic things. Spiritually I just use to question my God, like why is he so good to my sister but not to me? I think my life would be worse if my father was in it fully. He's toxic to me most of the time so it's not like I'll gain anything positive from it. He made the choice to be in and out of my life, for what reason I'll probably never understand. I used to blame myself and my mom for him not wanting to be involved when I was younger, but I came to the realization that he's a grown man and people are gonna have to deal with their mistakes at the end of the day. He never once admitted to his mistakes and I don't think he ever will. He used to have power over me when I was a preteen but now I feel I have power over him.

Since I'm doing good now he tries to be more active and engaged. I never wanted to be seen as a victim because I conquered without him, graduated without him, and a real man took his place. Like my stepfather always told me since I was 13, "Every action has a consequence." My action was living my life and not letting him hold me back. Now he has to deal with the consequence.

Anonymous

Diary: my daddy's scar:

My mom had me during her senior year of high school and she and my dad have been in an off and on relationship since then. I don't really remember my dad being around for me when I was younger. From what I recall, it's always been my mom and I until my brother was born, when I was 7 years old. My dad cheated on my mom when I was about 10 years old. We were on our way to church when my mom realized that she didn't have her bible. When we went back home to get it, my dad was in the house with another woman. My brother was too young to understand anything that was going on but I watched as everything unfolded around me. When I was in middle school, my brother and I moved out with my mom into an apartment. At 14, my little sister was born but my parents' relationship was still rocky. Amid everything that was going on, we moved back home with dad but within a few months, we moved out again. At this point, we had been bouncing from home to home for years, so I grew accustomed to random changes in my life.

I was active in school but my dad never really showed his face at any of my performances. I made A's and B's but even then, it felt like nothing I ever did was good enough to satisfy him or make him appear. I would come home with my report card, but he never seemed satisfied at the high marks. I felt so much pressure to be perfect for him. Even though we didn't see eye to eye, I secretly wanted to be better because I felt that maybe he would want to be more involved in my life. I never had someone to attend daddy-daughter functions with, take me out on dates, or show me how a man should treat a woman. I never really thought about how these things would affect me. When I would hang out at my friends' house, I would always get jealous as I watched them interact with their fathers. I felt like a piece of my heart was missing and I always wanted to know what it felt like to have unconditional love. How

would my life be if my dad really wanted me? I felt like he wasn't there for me like he was for my brother and sister. I felt like I was abandoned by him. I wondered, "What was wrong with me? Why doesn't he want me? Why am I getting treated differently?"

My mom worked as a pediatric nurse, shift 8-5, and sometimes 8-6 every day, all year round. When she worked in the summer, I had to watch my siblings. It put a lot of pressure on me because I was responsible for taking care of them. I learned to be independent and responsible because I didn't want to rely on my mom and I wanted to help out as much as I could because I knew being a single mom of 3 kids wasn't easy.

Growing up I had a lot of responsibility and I often felt alone. I couldn't talk to my mom because I could tell she felt like she was caught in the middle and didn't want to pick a side. I never wanted her to "choose" me. I wanted her to hear me out and try to understand how I felt. I attended a local dance studio where I took classes every week. Every year at the spring recital, they had an optional father daughter dance. My mom would always push me to do it with him but I really didn't want to. I knew it would be too uncomfortable for me. To me he wasn't my father... he was more of a stranger. I was also on the drill team at my high school. Every year during football season, there was a dance called, "Bob and Sue," and they would teach us a dance and our fathers had the chance to dance with us on the football field. My first two years on the team, my dad danced with me and it felt like the longest three minutes of my life. It just felt so fake and staged. My senior year my dad stood me up for "Bob and Sue" and I had to ask my principal to dance with me. I remember my heart racing as I stood on the sidelines on the field not knowing if he would show. I was so embarrassed and I tried to figure out what I would tell my teammates when they asked why I was dancing with the principal. My drill team also had a spring show called, "Stellar Revue." The second half of the show was dedicated to the graduating seniors. They also had a father

daughter dance as well. I talked to my dad about performing with me so I assumed that he was going to show up. As time passed throughout the show, I began to panic because I wasn't sure if he was there or not. I texted my mom and asked her was he in the audience but I didn't getting a response. I texted my boyfriend and asked if he could ask his dad to fill in. I didn't have time to wait for a text back because I was next on stage. If it had not been for my boyfriend's dad, I would've went on stage and been embarrassed to find out that my dad could not perform with me. He didn't even come to the show. I tried to bottle up my emotions, but inside I was really disappointed and angry. When I got home that day, my dad came in my room hugging on me. I went crazy.

"Get off of me!" I said.

I couldn't believe that after he just stood me up, he had the audacity to come and act like nothing ever happened. Whenever we got into a disagreement, he would always go run and tell my mom instead of addressing me like any other "father" would. The next day, my mom wouldn't even speak to me. I knew that he had told her what happened last night after the show. I was so confused. Why was she mad at me? How am I wrong in this situation? I wasn't surprised though. Anytime he told her anything, instead of coming to me and asking me what happened, she always reacted off what he told her. My grandmother noticed the tension between my mom and I and she started asking questions. I told her what happened and my mom said that she thought that I knew that he wasn't going to be at the show. After I told her he never let me know that he wasn't going to be there, her response was simply, "Oh. I thought he told you."

I could not believe that she was being so mean to me when she didn't even come and ask my side of the story. That's how things were back then. It felt like she finally chose a side. We never spoke about what happened. I was walking on pins and needles around the house. My mom always expected me to speak to my dad first and if I didn't, I would get in trouble. If he didn't speak to me, she

wouldn't say anything. I just felt like things weren't ever going to change. It only seemed as if they were getting worse. I started dating my boyfriend in 2013. I believe that God placed him in my life at the perfect time. He was the perfect gentlemen and best friend. He became the person that I would go to when I felt like nothing was right. I was able to confide in him anytime things were going wrong at home. That was a big step for me because throughout the years, I had kept all of my feelings to myself.

His dad also plays a major part in my life. He began to treat me like his own daughter and he hadn't even known me that long. I watched the way that he interacted with his daughter and it made my desire for that father-daughter love grow stronger. He took me under his wing and did things that my biological father didn't do for me. I wondered, how is it that someone who has only known me for a few years could treat me like such a princess? Although he was there for me in many ways that my own dad was not, it still didn't fill that void that was in my heart.

A few months after my dad stood me up, we got into a huge altercation one day when he was taking me to work. While we were in the car he kept picking with me until something triggered inside of me. He told me how I'm so disrespectful towards him and how I'm only repeating what I've been taught. (When in reality my mom has never taught me to disrespect him nor do I feel that I disrespect him in any way). I kept trying to ignore him but after a while I couldn't take it anymore.

"I'm so sick of you!" I screamed. "Another man had to take your spot on stage because you stood me up and you act like nothing ever happened!"

We continued to exchanged words back and forth before I got out of the car. I was filled with so many emotions. I couldn't even work because I was crying so hard. I had never talked to my dad like that and that was the first time that I honestly told him how I felt. My manager sent me home because I was just all over the place. I

wasn't really sure what was going to happen to me when my mom found out. After she and I sat down and I told her what happened. I was shocked by her response. She told me that my dad didn't know how to show his love for me because his parents weren't really good at expressing their love for him. She also said that the reason he treats me differently than my brother and sister is because when I was born, he was a 17 year old boy who still wanted to run the streets. She told me that no matter what, she expects me to do right by him and love him even if he doesn't love me in return. How is it my fault that he wanted to run the streets after I was born? Why should I be punished for that? I would think that he would want more for his children if he knows what it feels like to have a parent who isn't there for you. After my mom and I talked, we never spoke of the incident again. We just swept it under the rug like it never happened. It bothered me when my dad would try and take credit for my accomplishments, like he was the one there teaching, guiding, and molding me into a woman. My mom is the reason I was able to dance on every stage, arena, and football field that I stepped my foot on. My mom is the reason we traveled to Orlando, Florida for free to attend the Disney Dreamers Academy. My mom is the reason I graduated in the top 25% of my class. Not him.

Now that I'm in college my dad and I don't speak at all. He doesn't call and neither do I. My mom always pushed me to call him, but it seemed like every time we talked, we couldn't hold a conversation without arguing so I just stopped calling because I wanted to avoid that. I'm lucky if I even get a 'Happy Birthday' text.

My first year away from home was really hard for me as far as dealing with the drama that came along with my dad. I realized that I was a daddy-less daughter when I was doing a self change assignment for my professor, Mrs. Wiggins. The purpose of the assignment was to pick something that you wanted to change about yourself or your life and track it with a chart. At the end of the

semester, I had to create a three-minute video about the goal. As a part of my self healing process, I attended counseling on campus. That was my first time ever talking to someone outside of my family about what was going on in my life. It was very therapeutic for me. The title of my self-change video was, "I Am a Daddy-Less Daughter." At my graduation party, I created a fifteen-minute slideshow of memories with my family and friends. I only had about three pictures with my dad and I and I didn't have any pictures with his mom or any of his other family. Can you imagine how he felt as he watched it?

Miyah Gibson

Journal Entry #1:

A phenomenal, strong, and intelligent woman. I am. I be.
I introduce myself in such ways because I am a daddyless daughter; however, being a daddyless daughters does not define who I am. It does not take away the 20 years of hard work and achievements.
I am aware of who my father is, but as of right now we do not have a relationship. My dad is a revolving door dad, coming in and out of my life as he has pleased. I noticed that it is part of a cycle because his father was not in his life either. I really wouldn't classify his father as my grandfather because I can count on both hands the number of times I've seen him throughout my entire lifetime. The man whom my grandmother is married to today and has been so for almost 40 years now is my grandfather. I value the relationship I have with him because he took me in as if I was his own.
The moment I realized that my dad was not going to be in my life was when I wrote him "that letter." My dad had gone to jail, and at that time I still fought for my relationship with him. In the letter I informed him that everything was going to be alright. God was going to bring him out of every situation, and many more words of encouragement. Our relationship had been somewhat okay. I visited him in jail and he gave me a lot of what I came to know as jail talk. They tell you that whenever they get out, they're going to be a better person. He told me that he was going to continuously be a part of me and brothers' lives.
It never happened. I had poured so much of my heart in "that letter" and for him to lie to me hurt. Even when people were beginning to give up on him, I was the only one being positive and trying to give him a chance. I just don't understand how you can just look someone in the face and feed them all this bs and then you don't make the effort to make anything happen. But I guess that's why it's called bs, right?

Most of what I remember from my parent's relationship really was more negative than positive. My father was verbally and physically abusive to my mother. From what people told me they were high-school sweethearts and this and that, but people grow and people change. I am proud of my mother for being such a strong individual by leaving that marriage. It takes a strong person to do such things because most women stay for the sake of their children or because they're scared. But not my mom. She is my queen, and she has sacrificed so much for my brother and me in so many ways. She is caring, nurturing, and loving and I wouldn't want to ask for any other mother because she is my world.

My mom and I are literally best friends, it is so crazy! If I'm having a bad day she knows it, if I'm sad, in a crazy mood, or angry, she knows it. I grow closer to her every day because I appreciate everything that she does. Everything that she told me while I was younger, I am starting to understand how and why she went about things. My mom used to be strict. She didn't let me do anything. I thank her for that because I could have been wild and all over the place but she molded me to be a go-getter, independent, and strong just like her.

My grandfather became the male figure in my life. When I tell you they don't make anyone like my grandfather anymore they really don't. This is my mother's father, and he and my grandma have been married for over 40 years. He provided and took care of us. He always gave us the truth even if it hurts.

I've recently been talking to this guy for some time now and he has showed me much more than any guy I've ever dated. He shows me that I should never be treated anything less than what he is giving to me. I am so thankful for him because he makes me feel beautiful, he makes me smile when I am having a bad day, he's respectful, and anything and everything I could ever ask in a man. Something that my father lacked.

I've only been in two relationships and the relationships that I was

in were long term. I was on and off with my first relationship for about three years, and my second for two. I'm not going to lie, I have been naïve at time with guys but since a real man has come into my life and introduced me to what a real man should be, not anymore. I don't expect anything less from anyone else. I was in the relationships for so long because I couldn't accept how to be myself, and did not like being with myself which lead to me having low self-esteem. I couldn't accept how to fully love myself so I found that validation within relationships, when I should have been finding it within myself. January of this year I did. I started my weight loss journey, and before then I began to grow closer with my relationship with God. I had to take out time for myself and realize what was best for me, which was me. Honey when I tell you I know I am a baddie, I am a baddie and I own that "baddiness" to the highest potential.

I would just like to say that for those fathers who have daughters and are not present in their lives, you should start soon. You being a father starts the blue print, the foundation of your little girl's life. You are her first love, and when you don't show up in her life it could cause problems, such as low self-esteem, abandonment issues, trust issues, lust, everything that is self-destructive to your daughter. However, daddyless daughters, if your father is not present in your life, do not let it dictate your life. Yes, you are a daddyless daughter, yes, you might have some issues, yes, it will take a lifetime to heal but you cannot let that hold you back from your blessings. You do not have to be stuck on the "what if's" in your life. If you want to do something do it, if you want to be something be it. Yes, your father might not be in your life, but The Heavenly Father will never leave you nor forsake you!

Being a daddyless daughter has taught me so much. It gave me ambition, perseverance, strength, dedication, and most importantly it drove me to the Lord. When I tell you that God is good, and that he works miracles trust and believe me he does. God is my father,

and he is a great father. He picks me up when I'm down, he gives me joy, peace, happiness, anything you name it, God is that. He loves me even when I'm doing wrong and I thank Him for that. I thank God for allowing me to go through certain situations in my life because I would not be the woman who I am today. I do not consider myself a victim of the situation because I don't dwell on being a daddyless daughter, this is my success story honey. Because if you think about it, more positives came out of my life than negative. Honey, you got to pick yourself up, wear that crown, and make something of yourself. Look at me, I am a sophomore at Prairie View A&M University. I was blessed enough to have both of my years paid for without any loans. I've had the experience of traveling, meeting people, making boss moves, experiencing new things and opportunities and I am in an organization designed to help women like me. Can you say blessed? Your girl is really out here flourishing and growing and I am so proud of myself. I could have been pregnant at 16 but I'm not. I could have been fast but I'm not. I didn't have to go to school but I did. I beat the odds. I am not a statistic. That's why it is imperative that girls like me in similar situations think of their positives more than their negatives because nine times out of ten the good will out weight the bad. And trust me God will not put more on you than you can bear. So ladies, you go out there and be the greatest, most beautiful, and intelligent woman you can be! Do not let your past dictate your future. Stay strong, stay patient, and stay loved.

Signed The Phenomenal, Strong, and Intelligent Woman.

Miyah Gibson

Anonymous

April 1,
As a child, I realized that my household was different than others. My mother was a senior in high school when she had me. My parents got married and had their second child when I was three years old. We moved to Virginia for a year, then moved back home. I was five and my brother was two when they separated. I don't remember anything about my dad. I still became close with my grandpa, so he became my father figure. Everything my dad didn't do my grandpa always did for me. My grandpa played a major role in my life. He supported me in all the sports I played. He came to the majority of my birthday parties, graduation, and performances. My grandpa never let me down. He always pitched in to help my mother and my siblings. He claims that all of my siblings but three are not biologically his grandkids, yet he still loved them. My mother now has five children in total. After my mother had my brother she met another guy. They were together for a little while, then she had my other brother. Their relationship didn't last long though.

April 2,
When my mother became a police dispatcher it required her to work long, stressful hours so my two brothers and I stayed with my granny a lot. Eventually my mother met a guy that worked as a fireman at the same department as she did. The only thing that became an issue was that he was married and had children that he lived with. In order to keep their secret relationship going, one of them had to leave their job to prevent any issues. This led to my mother becoming a stay at home mom. Later she found out that she was pregnant with my little sister and soon enough so did his wife. His wife became angry and would call my mother's phone and sometimes show up at our apartment when my brothers and I were at school. At the time my siblings and I were too young to

understand what was going on. I was a very curious child, so I did notice that there was something weird going on. I would overhear my mother's conversations. My mom began to really fall for this guy. I knew that this was my mom's boyfriend, but she wanted us to call him dad, which was weird because I didn't feel like he was my dad. I just called him that without questioning her because I knew it would make her happy. After my sister was born things were still the same, but I always thought that it was weird how he would come over every other day. Why didn't he live with us? I thought to myself.

April 3,
Two years later, my mom became pregnant again by the same guy. I'm not sure if the wife knew about my youngest sister. As I grew older I realized that he played a huge role in our lives. He is wealthy. Not only was he a fireman, but he is a preacher, city council, and owns more than one business with his wife. He provided us with school clothes, cars, food, and anything else that we needed. I feel like there were times that he made my mom emotionally stressed and drained. My mom goes through depression. She has gained weight and sheltered herself in her room. Sometimes I feel like if she wanted him out of her life, but I feel that she feels like she needs him financially, so she won't let us down. She tries her hardest to provide for us.

April 4,
I attended the same high school as his two daughters did. I always wondered if they knew who I was because I knew exactly who they were. I was praying they didn't know what was going on. I knew it would have hurt their family emotionally. During my senior year in high school, I was getting ready for college. This is when my biological dad was slowly trying to help with funds and he started to call more often. Still to this day my father and I won't have a bond that a daughter and father should have. I love my father to death.

Without him and my mother I wouldn't have the chance to become the person I am now. I'm not angry at my father. I just always wanted to know why he didn't try as hard to see me grow up and be more supportive as he should. My father has three children, two boys and I am his only daughter. He hasn't been in any of our lives. I feel that his drug abuse did have something to do with part of us not having a relationship. My father was also in and out of jail a couple of times. Why? I wouldn't know, my family really kept the negative things about my father out of my life. I wished I knew more about my dad. It sucks to watch him grow older over a Facebook page.

Dezarae Johnson

~ ~ ~

Dezarae's Diary,

Let me just be real and say I don't really feel like my story is a story to move anyone positively. I feel like it is the unreleased version of all the anger and hurt that has been built up inside of me and part of what made me this cold, quick to cut you off, push you away type story. The type of story you can just nod your head in agreeance to and say, damn, I feel that. Whoever is reading this, I hope you find enough strength in yourself to someday tell your own story, regardless of what you feel it is or isn't, as long as it IS and that's all that matters.

To give you a little background about the person writing this story, my name is Dezarae Johnson, and I am a senior Health major from Waco, Texas, attending Prairie View A&M University. I am half Hispanic and Black. My mother is Hispanic, and my father is Black. I have a total of 11 siblings, 4 of whom are deceased due to either a premature birth or suffering a short life. Both my mother and father have three different people they have had children with (including themselves as a unit).

As you know, you are reading the story of a Daddyless Daughter. For those who aren't aware, there are five types of fathers defined by the organization: Revolving Door Father (In and out of life by choice), Shadow Father (present physically, but not involved mentally, emotionally and spiritually), (MIA) Missing in Action Father, Misplaced Father (unknown or never present), and Angel Father (Deceased). I am the Daddyless Daughter of the MIA kind.

At age two and half, my father went to jail for a robbery case for seven years. As a free man, for a small time in the past and present, he claims that him being a loyal person led him to make the decision to get in a car with friends who he had no idea had just robbed a bank. I question this explanation, yet, I cannot speak on

something I was not there to experience. Quite frankly, it sounds like an answer coming from a man who sticks to his story, which is exactly the kind of man my father is. Stick to your story regardless if it is a lie. And then you can't deny that gut feeling that tells you, "Don't believe that shit"!

My father returned to my life as a free man again when I was nine. By this time, my mother was dating two guys (In my explanation for her, she was seeing who the best candidate was to be a true man that would take the responsibility of 'raising' her kids and love her and them all in one. At the time it was just me and my sister Keyana). Let me just say this: out of the entire time my mother has raised me I have only seen her involved with the three men who she has produced children for. Anybody else faded away for whatever reason—something not meant for me to understand nor is it my business. As a kid I remembered them by either the one that always bought us kids candy or the one who called us "baby," which I thought was gross. One night, my mother, the guy who always bought us candy, my sister and I went to the store. When he went in the store my mother looked over her shoulder at us and asked, somewhere along these lines: "Who should I choose girls"? She said it with a smile, a small chuckle, and a hint of seriousness all in one. Me being me, I said the one who buys us candy. Little did I know it was going to turn out to be pure hell from that point on. Don't get me wrong, we had good times with my step father, but it's always those negative times that leave the biggest impact. I remember thinking while my dad was incarcerated, here came someone into our lives that I knew was not my daddy, which meant I wasn't going to let him tell me what to do, how to do it, when to do it or where to do it. Yet, I was also willing to accept the candy, the gifts, the fun side and everything else positive, but I'll be damned if he had any say-so when it came to issuing out demands to Dezarae Justine Johnson. I wish my biological would realize that because he was gone I had to deal with the idea and reality of another man raising

me. I always wanted my parents to be together and I never could understand why I couldn't have that fairy tale life that Disney Channel falsifies you to believe that you'll have with the damn white picket fence, overprotective and energetic mom that comes and supports all your games with a dad who sits you on his lap and calls you princess and beautiful. The kind of dad who tells you everything about the mind of a boy when they tell you to your face they care for you but by appearance only one thing touches the forefront of his mind or the tip of his "jimmy" and that's your poo-nanny, your hidden jewels, your sacred diamond. I think that's what pisses me off the most is that back when my memory can retain moments when my dad was affectionate with me, just loving on me like his only love child, that he disappeared and while my mama is my A-1, my soul, rock and anything that describes strong, my mama is not affectionate whatsoever. But that inaffectionate trait is a real representation of how a person can't give you what they weren't given themselves. My mom's mom wasn't affectionate with her, so domino effect here we are.

That's the part I was missing from a father, that affectionate love that assures you no boy can break and that even when a man approaches, you know that no matter how much you love that man, that he'll never replace your father. I don't care if I and Boaz get married and it's been said that my husband and I have to become one like that's my daddy that set the bar before you, tuh! But I didn't have that, which left me feeling like I was ready for someone, anyone to show me the same attention my father would show me in the spurts. I started looking for it in boys, then friends, then it trickled all the way down to everyone. I felt like I needed everyone's approval and that I couldn't make it in life without it. I remember seeing so many girls with boyfriends and wondering why I couldn't have one. What was wrong with me? Was I too ugly? Did I not dress good enough? What made everyone else girlfriend material and not me? What was special about them? One thing I can say I

got from my father was protection and now I realize that in the relationships I allow to happen are the ones that involve the man being my protector and if he can't be that it doesn't matter what he can bring to the table, he's just not good enough. Between my dad's endless stories of prison fights and murders, it gave me a sense of security that if anyone were to ever cross my daddy or me that he would have to deal with us both and that nobody could touch me if they tried. That's the happy part I remember. But my father not being there was a constant reminder of the poverty I lived in, the statistics people put on me, first seeing me as another black child without a father present to raise his daughter, the kind of life my mother and I were limited to. My mind was always on if my father would have kept his promise to my mother and I that he would be there that I would have lived a better life in growing up, that I would be secure in my beauty inside and out, that I would have went to private school, you know the kind that costs a lot of money but helps in the end because of the education they provide, that I would have more confidence and wouldn't need nobody to validate me or who I am. I feel like I was robbed of love, robbed of a better childhood, robbed of time and robbed of the little girl who could accept the word "promise" cause I sure as hell don't! In fact, I hate when people use the word "promise" in anything cause I'd rather you tell me that you'll keep your word to me rather than possibly breaking a promise like my father did. But then I think about the strength I have today and how far God allowed me to make it and I think had my father been in my life to spoil me with gifts and love that, "yeah, I'd have great attributes about myself"! But I also think would I carry a strong weight on my shoulders without folding? Would I guard my heart with a particular preciousness because I never had a man or my biological father to show me how a man is supposed to treat his lady, so I fall less, I guess? All I know is Daddyless Daughters are one of a kind! Our first and second father is the Lord, the God Almighty, He is all that for the man who

couldn't be there when we needed him, for the man who couldn't show us the love that we desired; to be the apple of our father's eyes, for the man who couldn't tell you the game and how boys would run it on you, for the man who didn't or still doesn't realize that his absence left his daughter to take on a weight that she didn't bargain for. The kind of weight that's heavy when she walks amongst girls who had or have their fathers in their life, the heavy weight of the cloud of insecurity that follows her everywhere she goes because she feels lost and that a part of her is missing. There's always questions that haven't been answered or never will be that roam around in my mind. As I bring my testimony to a close that still has an ending unwritten and put out into the world, thanks for listening to my soul cry.

Love,

Dezarae Justine Johnson, Daddyless Daughter

Amber
41 year old South Texas Gal

My Pink Diary:

They say that we're a myth, but we're real. They say we don't exist, but we are a dent in history. The media never truly show us, not like they should. Perhaps there has been a movie or two about us, maybe a reality show even (I can't recall) but it went exempt from the stereotyping of us all. I'm not a stereotype, but I'm also not okay.

I once saw an old TV show, *One Day at a Time*, where the father wasn't in the home. The overall perception I took from it, is that it was just an anaomaly, not to be taken seriously, not to be taken as part of white family culture, not to be viewed as the psychologically destructive force that it is. I immediately knew that this wasn't a negative or stereotype on white fathers as compared to *What's Happening*, and the absent father in that show. Or, two of my favorite shows, *Married With Children* and *Just Shoot Me!* In *MWC*, the father is like a CPS worker's dream, but it's just comedy to America so we ignored the lack of love and neglect and laughed at it. In *JSM*, again, it was okay because the father gives the daughter a job and helps her out of a financial bind so we ignore the hurt he caused during her childhood that they even bring up ever so often and we don't judge him harshly because still, he makes us laugh. That is the ugly part of the white privilege we enjoy, a privilege that leaves many of us cold and uncovered, shivering in a house with no lights.

So the media continues to bury our existence, making it harder and harder for us to heal from our tragedy. They won't tell our story so we have to tell it ourselves, even if it's just to you diary...

~~

I grew up in South Texas in a small town. Even though I was a cute child, I wanted to be a tomboy, so I hung out with my male cousins

a lot, following them around wherever they went and rarely revealing my cuteness. It helped that my dad wanted a boy for a child so getting the clothes was a cinch.

I loved my dad growing up, but he was a victim of the 1980s crack wave, so to keep loving him was kind of hard to do over time. He was discreet about it in the beginning, wanting to avoid the backlash and shaming that he'd done to his family. Discreet in order to maintain a semblance of fatherhood. But if anyone has or know a parent who is addicted to crack, then they can tell you that the two don't mix.

I have many memories of my dad; some of them are good; most of them are awful, beginning with him showing up drunk to my 10th birthday party. He was supposed to be a clown, a surprise I'd overheard my parents discussing. But he stumbled through the door late, dressed not as a clown but as the neighborhood wino, giving everybody a true surprise. He reeked of whiskey, cursed all of the kids because he'd forgotten why they were there, and ask my mom about his dinner. The party went on, without the clown. My dad griped from the bedroom until he passed out. As a joke, I thought it'd be funny if me and some of the other kids snuck into his room and smeared cake on his face. Usually, that would have resulted in a whipping but when he woke, he was discombobulated, so he didn't know if he had done it to himself or not. It was one of the few things I got away with.

After I turned 11, his crack addiction outgrew and became more powerful than his love for his family. I believe he meant well, but that drug is stronger than most folks imagine. My back never had a monkey so it would be hard for me to say that he should have just quit, even though a man's family should come before any drug. My mom never got monkey-on-your-back hooked, but she dabbled in it enough to satisfy him and continued to dabble in it to keep the family together, but the drug was doing the opposite. Only I could

see that. The first time I walked in on them my dad beat me, perhaps shocked and not knowing what else to do. Every subsequent time he would just yell and tell me to go watch cartoons or fix myself something to eat or go play with my cousins. My mom would always have this look on her face as if she was embarrassed, a look that followed me to bed.

~~

Whenever my cousins and I got into it, they would tease me, saying my dad is a basehead and that they'd seen him selling my bike for a piece of dope. I never had a comeback for them. I would leave and either go home or to the park to play by myself or with someone else. Cousins are mean, but they are also caring. They would always apologize to me and we would be okay until the next spat.

Once, I found my dad's crackpipe and I threw it in the garbage. He was watching me the entire time. For my punishment, he dumped all the garbage onto the floor and made me pick every bit up, discarded food and all, with my hands.

Sometimes I made money by helping the neighbors clean their house or walk their dogs. I kept the money in my piggy bank on my dresser. Whenever he was short of money, my dad would always go into my piggy bank and remind me with his belt of whose house this was, who paid the rent, who put clothes on my back, and who fed me. Mom used to intervene, but after a few months her main focus was keeping dad happy, nothing else. Guess that's what love can do to a person. Then little by little, my room started to be cleared of all my good stuff, my Atari, my Walkman, another bike that one of the neighbors had given me for helping them so often. I kept it in my room because I thought he wouldn't dare sell it if it was in there. I knew about this one before my cousins.

I had what I call mini runaways, where I would leave for four to five hours without anyone knowing of my whereabouts because I had become fed up with dad. I don't believe he even missed me because

whenever I would walk back in he would just tell me to wash dishes after I was done eating. If he wasn't there, then mom would ask me where I'd been, off-handedly, and maybe we'd play games if she was in the mood. Since she had started dabbling more with dad, mom was rarely in the mood to deal with me like before.

I felt sorry for her, because even then, I knew she didn't want to do that drug. It was all because of dad. But she continued to dabble, through me being 11, through 12, and most of 13 until she was the victim of a hit and run down the block from the crackhouse.

When mom passed I stayed with dad for a while. He wasn't in any shape to take care of himself, let alone a child. It wasn't long before utilities started getting cut off. I started stealing because I wanted to eat. I stole so much that I wasn't allowed at any of my friends' houses. When I got caught stealing from stores, my favorite was Brookshire Bros., dad would put on this big front in front of the cops like he couldn't understand why I would do such a thing, then whip me naked when they left. I didn't mind the whippings much, not at this point. It was either starve or steal. Besides, I was getting better at it and wouldn't be getting caught as often. My cousins started teaching me a few tricks to make myself less obvious.

A couple months after my mom passed, our house had become empty. Most of the stuff we'd had, dad had sold for crack rock. He rented his car out a lot too and sometimes the men wouldn't bring it back on time so if I ever missed the bus to school, I had to walk.

I watched my dad night after night bring different people into the house, his smoking buddies. He even moved a woman in, but only for a month. He kicked her out when she took some of his stuff without his permission. He tried to make me think she was one of my distant cousins.

The summer of 1989 my dad told me that we would lose our house. I asked him where we would move to and he said that he would stay with a friend and that maybe I could ask one of my aunts to let

me move in with them for a while. I never did because I was embarrassed. Instead, he just dropped me off at my mother's youngest sister one day like he would be back in a couple of hours and never returned. Three days later, he snuck my clothes over at night and left them on the porch.

My aunt assured me that it was alright for me to stay with her and that I wouldn't have a thing to worry about. I trusted her. She never lied to me her whole life. What I didn't trust was her ability to keep her promise due to her finances. My aunt had five children, two male cousins around my age (one the same, the other one year older. We were all three in the same grade.) Two were merely babies, two years (a boy) and the youngest (a girl) just under one year. The oldest cousin was a girl by four years older than I was and she didn't like me or her siblings much. She had a boyfriend and had been pregnant once, moved out, lost the baby, moved back home with her boyfriend staying there most of the time. My aunt's husband didn't have a regular nine to five job. He was what we called a nomad worker. Sometimes he worked in the woods cutting trees, sometimes he hauled junk, sometimes he pawned things. At least he helped out, and he treated his wife and kids with kindness and love. Me too, as much as he could.

My aunt worked at a small restaurant, small only in size, but brought in pretty good profit. If she had a full time working husband and maybe three less kids, my aunt would have been lower middle class. That's what I think about when I was added to her brood. A little misfit child, motherless by death, fatherless by drugs. How could she love me in her already full house after the initial honeymoon session is over is what I kept wondering? I kept waiting, one week, three weeks, one month, two months, five months. My aunt kept loving me and making me feel welcomed though I felt unwelcomed. I helped out around the house often, feeling it was my duty as the outsider. I did my cousins' chores for them often, and even won the favor of the oldest because I lied for

her a lot. Sometimes she would give me a dollar for lying, other times she would promise not to beat me up.

So, life afer being abandoned by my dad started off alright. I had good cousin friends, an aunt who loved me like a mom, even with five of her own, and an uncle who did what he could to make me feel like the natural sixth child.

~~

I was the subject of much ridicule as a freshman in high school. I mean, my background made me easy pickings. I got into so many fights that the school was forced to keep me in in-school detention for a while. They didn't want to. They gave me multiple chances, but after I pulled a teacher's hair I had played their hand. My aunt couldn't understand why I was fighting so much, even more than my cousins, sometimes with them. She didn't understand; the teachers didn't understand; the principle didn't understand. But I did. I was jealous at everything and everybody and I wasn't going to tell anyone about it either.

One day I skipped school bcause I didn't feel like sitting in that one detention room all day. I went to the tracks, the easiest place to skip because no lawmen ever came through there. There were always box cars or a caboose sitting there unused. It's a place I went to with my cousins maybe only once or twice per month, not too big a part of our childhood. This day I was just going to sit in the caboose until I saw the school bus pass.

To my surprise, when I climbed in my dad was in the caboose with a woman. She was half naked. I could tell that they'd been smoking. I knew how his eyes would become like this yellowish-red and his mouth would be drawn in. I argued with the woman about why I wasn't in school and who had the right to be in the caboose.

My dad found our back and forth amusing, finally saying, "This here, this is my daughter." The woman made a face and stopped

arguing with me. She started rubbing on my dad's inner thigh and he let her.

Then they smoked in front of me. I think my dad wanted to mess with me in that caboose. He never said it or made a move but the way I caught him looking at my body or the way he and the lady made out in front of me said otherwise. As a child you know, It doesn't always have to be a physical action. I could only turn around when he was revealed.

We sat in that caboose until their high wore off. Then they left. I asked my dad for a dollar but he said he didn't have it. I knew then that the situation with him was permanent.

The day after my fourteenth birthday I ran away, this time for real. It rained that day, beginning around ten that morning. A quiet and grey Sunday morning. I packed a small bag quietly and snuck out the bathroom window around 5pm. Most everybody there was napping, giving me enough time to get far away before I would be missed. I had no reason to run away. My aunt and uncle were good to me, I enjoyed the company of my cousins, I liked staying at my aunt's house. I only ran away this time because of the attention it would bring from them. Being without parents, I sometimes required more.

I went and waited at the bathroom in the park for a while. The rain never stopped; it did let up some, but never completely stopped pouring. Before night fell I just grabbed my bag and walked down the city streets. People would only think I was out playing in the rain when they saw me. The only time I thought of getting shelter is when I first left, now I just roamed, not knowing or caring where I ended. I got splashed a couple of times by cars speeding by and finally a couple with a dog picked me up because it had gotten dark. They wanted to take me home but I wouldn't tell them where I stayed. They were nice people. Not knowing what to do with me, they took me to their house, hoping to get me to confess where I

lived or a number to reach someone. We ate dinner and watched TV. I took a bath and they both brought me a towel to dry off with. They were so nice. Usually, I would have cursed them out for coming in the bathroom like they did instead of leaving the towel by the door. If it were one of my boy cousins, we would have fought. But this couple was so nice. They had smiles on their faces when I climbed out the tub, trying to cover my privates. The woman said, "Don't be shy, you're a pretty girl." She helped me dry and then rubbed my shoulders. She grabbed me by the hand and led me into their bedroom where, under confusion and fear, the two of them shared me. They had to be no more than 25. I thought they were so nice for picking me up. They dropped me back off at the park by the slides and swings the next day without a word.

I blamed my dad for that night.

Scars #3

Michelle (#23)

My name is Michelle Jacobs. I'm a 40 year old, single parent of two beautiful children, Lorenzo Shelton and Jamaya Walker, and I'm from Richmond, California.

I loosely knew my father but I never got the chance to meet his parents or have a conversation with him about them. Therefore, I don't know if his father was in his life or if it made him the way he was—careless. I don't recall ever having my father in my life, maybe he was there as a baby, the times where human memory fails to flashback. I've only seen one baby picture of him. I was told the relationship between he and my mom was abusive, with a lot of drugs and alcohol involved.

Over the years, I have reflected on the relationship with my own mother and I don't believe my father being absent had anything to do with our our problems. They stemmed mostly from drugs, alcohol, and her abusive relationships with other men. My grandfather stepped-in and did what he could. However, I don't feel he made up for my father's absent and he also didn't teach me anything growing up.

The issues I have didn't come from being a daddyless daughter; they come from being a motherless daughter. As a child I missed a lot of school from moving around or taking care of my baby sisters while my mother ran the streets. I was a very angry child growing up because of this, until I moved in with my aunt Thelma.

Having kids at 16 and 19 is one of my biggest regrets, something that could have been done differently if my father was there—

perhaps. However, I don't, nor have I ever, desired a relationship with him at all. I'm coping well because I now understand that not everyone was or is ready to become a parent. I do believe that those who decide not to be a part of their daughter's life should just stay out; the back and forth only makes the emotional frustrations worse. Speaking from experience with my daughter, the worst thing is having an unstable man raise your daughter. So, regardless of what anyone thought, I kept her father away as much as possible. Sometimes it's best that men leave, especially if the relationship is unstable or abusive.

My life.

As a daddylesss daughter.

As a Motherless daughter.

I have a daughter.

I was afraid.

Not because of her father being absent, but because I didn't want to become a mother.

Life is full of critical decisions.

What did I learn? God doesn't make mistakes. God gave her to me.

Am I my daughter's keeper? God knows.

I know in my heart that I would probably be worse with the father of my children around. He is still unstable and doesn't have a relationship with his son. I've never asked him, but the very few conversations I've had, he blames my mother. I think he's a selfish man.

What has that caused?

Trust issues. Trust. Issues. It is nearly impossible for me to trust any man at all. My experience is, men just walk out when it's convenient for them, so I have to have total control of the friendship. I don't look for love in men. It's hard for me to believe anyone loves me.

No man has ever mistreated me other than my grandfather.

Men have to be the total opposite of my grandfather.

Men will walk out at any moment.

Be independent.
The bright side…
I was with a man for 14 years that gave my children unconditional love until the day he died.
What happened to my fear?
I'm so proud of my baby girl, the strong, beautiful, Jamaya Walker.

Scars #4

Jamaya Walker

'SHE TOLD YOU SO'

April 4, 2012:

Jason,
When you die
Your daughter isn't go remember you, she just gon'
remember your money.
Momma told you, but you didn't believe her.
When I was 5, I tried to tell you too.
Sitting in our apartment in Pinole,
I told my daddy,
"There's only two ways out of this game -
Death or prison for life,"
But you didn't believe me.
You told me you wouldn't end up like this
You told me you would leave the game before the streets took you -
You promised me…
But you were wrong
They took you daddy
The streets took hold of you
And the end result of your hustling days was death.
That memory replayed in my head like my favorite Lil' Boosie song.
As the cops put caution tape
Around my daddy's crime scene
And the gun shells that captured my daddy's precious soul
Laid beneath my size 9 shoes.

This is the life of a hustler's daughter.
Wait… No scratch that…

This is the life of a hustler's daughter,
Stepdaughter,
Niece,
Cousin,
Best friend, and
Girlfriend.
The life in which the smell of weed
Isn't an odor but a florescent fragrance.

The life of a little girl who's constantly paranoid
As her daddy disappears into the middle of the night
Only headed to the block - his other wife,
His true desire
The life of a little girl who's woken up at the crack of dawn
By her mom getting dressed heading to the hospital
Because her strength and pride as been shot.
You see, I was never your normal little girl.
I only played the role
Where momma would try to hide the truth
about where daddy was late at night,
But momma didn't realize I wasn't as gullible as she thought.
The look of pain told the truth about where daddy was.
The role where daddy would try to use
the hustler code on the phone,
because he thought I was too young to understand the
words that burned like ash from the tip of his blunt,
But really I could recite and define everything he just said
No stuttering
No hesitation
But I know the rules of the game
Snitches get stitches
You ain't seen nothing
You aint hear nothing
So I'd just bow my long pig tails and proceed to
eat the melting ice cream

daddy bought me while he did his transaction.
This is the life of a hustler's daughter
I was just preparing for this day.
The streets would catch up to him
How did I know it was going to end up like this?
Cold metal steal rather than cold metal bars
I just remember crying to daddy every day
Telling him he was go die in this game.
The street pole was the devil and the streets wasn't nothing
But a simple imitation of hell
Daddy was in denial.
Only telling me he would do whatever he had to do
To provide for his family.
If he had to hit the cold block every day to give his
little princess whatever she wanted
He would
If he had to whip up a few drugs in the kitchen just to keep his
son in the latest pairs of J's
He would
If he had to risk his life every day for 18 years just to keep his
family happy,
than that just what he was going do
Daddy, you put the streets before me but not intentionally.
At my daddy's funeral everybody stood around in their
R.I.P Jason shirts.
They told me to stop crying.
They told me think of all the good memorizes.
How the hell am I supposed to remember the good times
When there were none?
My daddy didn't come to anything that was important to me.
Not a cheerleading competition out of all the
10 years I been cheerleading
Not a school event,
Not a track meet,

Not anything
If anything,
I can remember the way that $100 bill felt
against the tip of my fingers
More than the way I could remember how his hand felt.
The only way I could remember his smell is if
I put on his old hoodie.
The only way I could remember his face is if
I look at his obituary.
I'm ashamed to say but it's the truth.
He grew up without everything he wanted
So he tried to give me everything I wanted
But everything he gave me
Wasn't everything I needed.
I didn't need
The money,
The shoes,
The unnecessary gifts.
It was a temporary distraction from his absence
Daddy
I needed you to learn how to tell me NO
I needed you to replace your money with your presence
Replace the time you spent in the streets
With the time you spent with me.
Momma told you that you would leave the wrong impression upon me
They say a girl looks for a boy just like her daddy
They say I become more and more like my mom every day
So daddy,
Does that mean Im'a look for a hustler who can buy me everything?
Who's constantly getting shot and shot at
Does that mean I will have to lie to my child about where her father is?
Will I have to cry myself to sleep wondering if he's alive?
Or do I deserve better?
When I was 5, I tried to tell you -

"Drug dealers either end up dead or in prison,"
But you wouldn't listen.
Shot in your leg twice when you were 18.
When I was 9, they held a gun to your head,
You were on your way to see me.
You said, "Don't kill me, I'm on my way to see my daughter."
The gun jammed.
Three strikes and you're out
Third time's the charm,
Like God's gonna keep sparing you
"I gave you warnings and you didn't listen,
Now it's time for you to come home."
The day you got killed
You were on your way to pick me up from Spanish class.
The gun didn't jam that time.
If you do something bad for a good reason do you still go to heaven,
because I always questioned my daddy's final destination
Momma tried to tell you but you didn't listen
The life of a hustler's daughter doesn't glisten
As bright as that ring you got her.
At night when I take off the clothes you bought me
I'm left naked, shakin',
Daddy, I miss you
And I wish you would've seen
Your money couldn't fill this whole in my heart
Only loved could do that
Only love.

From Jamaya Walker's upcoming autobiography

"Pour acid down my face
Letting it eat away at my flesh
Making me lose my identity
Rewind 15 years back and let the sperm backstroke to where it came from
Never letting it meet the egg that together would eventually create
me
Maybe the pain would go away
The pain of me knowing I am an offspring of you
Your body fluids make up part of my DNA
But you are no part of me"

Six years ago at the tender age of 15 I found myself feeling enslaved. Enslaved mentally, enslaved emotionally, enslaved spiritually and enslaved physically. Less than two decades into the world I was already being held captive by pain and anger. I sat, tears trickling down my brown sugar cheeks, whispering prayers to a God, who seemed to stop watching over me after He placed me in my mother's wound. I don't know which feeling of abandonment was worse...feeling like God had stopped protecting me or that he had stopped watching over me. No longer did I feel his presence in my room no matter how much I pleaded for him to come in; or was the realization of knowing "daddy" was gone more wounding? Momma said, "God doesn't hurt people." She said, "God never stops watching over his children." She hugged me and told me, "God loves me," but I felt different. I don't know who to blame for my broken heart or for the late nights I laid in bed, back to door, knees to chest with the only thing catching snot and tears were my pillow cases and bare hands. My tears, each holding a different question about my father. I mean deadbeat. I mean Jamar. His name is Jamar. The more questions that clouded my head, the faster my pillows turned into sponges, soaking up fragmented parts of me.

My computer lay beside me, through my blurry vision I read back the poem I had just written after staring at myself in the mirror for hours. I look like him. I look just like that man. That man who roams the same streets as me with my name engraved inside of his flesh but wants nothing to do with me. I guess he thought his tattoo could make up for his lost signature on my birth certificate. My mother's hate for that man during her pregnancy must have been as strong as iron as mine is now steel, and that's why I am a reflection of him. Momma says I am beautiful, but I look like the same person who took advantage of her, impregnated her and abandoned her. Though he wasn't the first man to turn his back on her a small part of me always felt like my mother's living nightmare. An everyday reminder to her of the con artist that swooped in, stole her trust, and then swooped out.

Momma was 19 years old when she became pregnant with me. She had my brother at 16, making me her second child.

But I was Jamar's first.

His first born child, born through the act of adultery.

Yes, I said it adultery.

My father, who is a few years older than my mother, failed to enlighten her that he had exchanged vows with a woman not too long before he met her. It's clear that he has a hard time committing to anything or anyone but I should have been different. I should have been the one girl to make him change. I am his first born child and his only daughter. I am the first person to have half of him. For the love of God, I am half of him! He was supposed to commit to me! Commit to loving me. Commit to protecting me. Commit to cherishing me and teaching me self-value and he didn't! He, like most little boys trapped in male bodies where I am from, have a hard time lying in the bed that they made. Jamar took the fastest route out my life taking a tattooed piece of me with him and leaving the rest with my momma.

Rage colonizes my heart when I think about how he took advantage of momma and left. She was already going through a lot at such a young age. My childhood is glitter and gold if you compare it to her upbringing. Introduced into the world in '77 she was born right before the highest level of downfall to the black family, right before the crack epidemic. During the late 70's and 80's most of the family was wrapped up in drugs and alcohol, including my granny, leaving momma to be raised by Big Granny, my great grandmother. May God rest her soul.

My grandfather? Well, my grandfather was on drugs with my granny and extremely abusive so he wasn't in my momma's life that long. Momma remembers the day she watched him backhand my granny right in front of her. That isn't anything new though. The women in my family marry men who like to play makeup artist. Have you ever seen a man highlight and contour a woman's face with his fist? Almost every woman in my family knows what it feels like to be beaten to the Gods by men who say they love them. Momma vowed to never blossom into those women and like most promises she makes she has never broken it.

Momma remembers the day my grandfather abandoned her and granny. He took everything with him and left them in an apartment with nothing but a lamp. It is one thing to turn your back on your family and it's another to turn your back and leave them with nothing to survive with. I will never understand how some men can do that. I know that day is the reason that, ever since I could remember, she has always told me, "Jamaya you don't depend on a man for anything. You do it yourself because the moment he gets mad he might take everything with him and leave you with nothing. So you always make sure you can afford to maintain the lifestyle you want with or without a man." No matter how much she tries to hide it, I know his leaving in the way he did as a child still hurts her. It was the first time a man turned his back on her and the seed that started the garden of trust issues, feelings of abandonment and

secret desires for affection. She and Granny stayed in that apartment for three days with nothing until my granny finally went to my Papa and told him what happened. Momma doesn't have great memories of her childhood. I have only seen very few pictures of her as a child. It was filled with pain, anger, and confusion.

Momma he had no plans on having a baby at the moment let alone a baby by a married man, she was already a single parent with a three-year-old son. The last thing she wanted to do was birth a child with a man who belonged to someone else so execution seemed to be the only option. God has a way of turning situations around and making a way out of no way because just when momma thought abortion was the only way, God sent her an angel on earth to change her mind. That angel was Jason Walker. My heart glistens when I think about him, the man who saved my life by putting an end to momma's abortion.

While working at Church's Chicken on McDonald Ave he came across momma while she worked the drive thru. High as a cloud, he ordered a 3 piece, side of fries with a large Orange soda. When he pulled up to the window something must have told him momma was the one for him because he was determined to have her. Resentment and unhealed wounds from men who claimed to have loved her resulted in him getting the cold shoulder. My grandfather left, my brother's father left, and my sperm donor left so she didn't trust a man for shit. My daddy's (Jason) green eyes didn't really help his case in trying to win her over either. They screamed hoe from a mile away. Picture this, light skin, drug dealer, green eyes, 6'2, gorgeous smile with a silent assassin demeanor. He could walk in a room and not say anything and you would know he was there. Every girl in Richmond wanted their hands on "green eyed Jason," but he wanted momma. He wanted momma even though she had already birthed a child and carrying another man's. He already had two children of his own—my oldest brother and my sister. Momma told him who my father was and how I came about but he did not

care. Richmond isn't that small so he knew who my birth father was and although he did not play a part in my creation you could not tell him anything about me. He in his heart believed I was his daughter and made a promise to my mother from that day forward he would be the father to me that Jamar chose not to be. He and Jamar are both from two opposite sides of Richmond, divided only by train tracks, Jamar from North Richmond while Jason was from the South side. Both of them were involved in the drug game. Both men from two opposite sides of town that are at war with each other still to this day. Both men, different views on life. Jamar, the leaver, who entered this life selfishly. Jason, the giver, who took me in as his own child and gave me his last name Walker and his middle name Lee.

Jason. Hamilton. Lee. Walker. Jason Hamilton Lee Walker.

Michelle Jacobs.

Jamaya Michelle Lee Walker.

A family.

After a glimpse of what life was like having a father it would soon come to an end. I would soon be a bastard twice over, a daddyless daughter twice over, a broken girl twice over. How does a girl cope with this? What do I do with my anger? Who is responsible for taking every man who was supposed to love me away from me? How do I cope with this desire for love? What happens to momma? This is the 3rd man snatched away from her.

Life is funny like that, where the good die young and the bad, most selfish individuals seem to live forever, to spread their hate to more people, to more decades, to more eras, to more generations.

Now Close the Diary

The brand. The name. The look. *Unspoken Words Of A Daddyless Daughter*. Jones House Publishing. Jamaya Walker.

Coming Soon: *Book 2: Unspoken Words From a Daddyless Daughter: Scars & Testimonies*

Also from Jones House Publishing:

The Women of Sugar Hill by Montayj

Street Tears by Montayj

New Orleans Shadows by Jazz Claiborne

Duggan by Montayj

Black-White Binaries of European Christianity and Colonialism by Montayj

The Journey Continues…

Follow Jamaya Walker, Changing My Destiny: Daddyless Daughters, and Jones House Publishing for updates and exclusives here at:

Instagram: @changing.my.destiny
@jamayamichelle
@jhpublishing

Facebook Fan Page: JH Publishing

www.WeBuyBlack.com: Jones House Store

If you enjoyed *Unspoken Words of a Daddyless Daughter*, please post a review at Barnes & Noble, iBooks, Smashwords, webuyblack.com, Amazon or other online retailers and visit our website and let your friends know about #DaddylessDaughters. #TeamJHP